D0801779

Isis and Osiris

EXPLORING THE GODDESS MYTH

DOUBLEDAY

New York

London

Toronto

Sydney

Auckland

ISIS

a n d

OSIRIS

EXPLORING THE GODDESS MYTH

JONATHAN
COTT

299.31
C

PUBLISHED BY DOUBLEDAY

a division of Bantam Doubleday Dell Publishing Group, Inc.
1540 Broadway, New York, New York 10036

DOUBLEDAY and the portrayal of an anchor with a
dolphin are trademarks of Doubleday, a division of
Bantam Doubleday Dell Publishing Group, Inc.

"The Mystery of the Awakening of Osiris" from *Dea: Rites and Mysteries of the Goddess* by Olivia Robertson
(Cesara Publications), used by permission of the author. © Olivia Robertson.

Photograph of Olivia Robertson and Lawrence Durdin-Robertson by Jeremy Nicholl. © Jeremy Nicholl
(Katz Pictures from Woodfin Camp & Associates, Inc.).

All quotations from *The Ammonite Way* (The 36 Lessons of the Ammonite Foundation), reprinted by
permission of the Ammonite Foundation. © The Ammonite Foundation.

Five pages from the Ammonite Calendar for the year 12,453 (1992), reprinted by permission of Sekhmet
Montu. © Sekhmet Montu.

Excerpt from "There Are No Gods," from *The Complete Poems of D. H. Lawrence*. Copyright © 1964, 1971
by Angelo Ravagli and C. M. Weekley, Executors of the Estate of Freida Lawrence Ravagli. Used by
permission of Viking Penguin, a division of Penguin Books USA, Inc.

Excerpts from *The Man Who Died* from *St. Mawr and The Man Who Died* by D. H. Lawrence. Copyright 1928
by Alfred A. Knopf, Inc. Reprinted by permission of the publisher.

Excerpts from *Ancient Evenings* by Norman Mailer. Copyright © 1983 by Norman Mailer. Reprinted by
permission of the author and the author's agents, Scott Meredith Literary Agency, Inc., 845 Third
Avenue, New York, NY 10022.

Excerpt from "Isis and Osiris" by Robert Musil from *Prosa, Dramen, Späte Briefe*, ed. by Adolf Frisé
(Rowohlt Verlag, 1957).

Drawings in Chapters 2, 7, and 8 by Mark Hasselriis, reproduced by permission of the artist.

Book design by Marysarah Quinn

Library of Congress Cataloging-in-Publication Data
Cott, Jonathan.
Isis and Osiris: exploring the goddess myth / Jonathan Cott. — 1st ed.
p.   cm.
1. Isis (Egyptian deity)—Cult—History.   2. Osiris (Egyptian
deity)—Cult—History.   I. Title.
BL2450.I7C68   1994
299'.31—dc20   93-3789
CIP

ISBN 0-385-41797-7
Copyright © 1994 by Jonathan Cott
All Rights Reserved
Printed in the United States of America
February 1994

1   2   3   4   5   6   7   8   9   10

First Edition

3 1764 00204 8274

For my mother

Who is it smooths the bedsheets like the cool
smooth ocean when the fishes rest on edge
in their own dream?

Who is it that clasps and kneads my naked feet, till
    they unfold,
till all is well, till all is utterly well? the
    lotus-lilies of the feet!

I tell you, it is no woman, it is no man, for I am alone.
And I fall asleep with the gods, the gods
that are not, or that are
according to the soul's desire,
like a pool into which we plunge, or do not plunge.

    —from "There Are No Gods," by D. H. Lawrence

Acknowledgments

I am inestimably grateful to my editor, Jacqueline Onassis, for guiding me through the realms of Isis and Osiris; to my agent, Michael Carlisle, for arranging my journey; and to the following persons who helped me on my way: Douglas Broyles, Heidi Draper, Liz Duvall, Isabel and Laura García Lorca, Cindy and Richard Gere, Diane Guzman (Wilbour Librarian of the Brooklyn Museum), Yasmine Hauri, Arville and Nancy Lester, Scott Moyers, Marysarah Quinn, Isabel Ruiz de la Prada, Manuela Wacha, Jane and Jann Wenner.

Contents

1

INTRODUCTION

*T*he world is filled with love stories, but few of them are as profoundly filled with as many facets of the world as the story of Isis and Osiris. Born of the God of the Earth and the Goddess of the Sky, Isis and Osiris—twin sister and brother—were said to have fallen in love inside their mother's womb. Not only sister and brother, they were also wife and husband, queen and king, goddess and god.

In the beginning, Osiris, whose presence was manifested in the sprouting grain and the rising waters of the Nile, invented agriculture, writing, and the arts, and transformed humanity from barbarism to civilization. Murdered and cut into fourteen pieces by his jealous brother Set, he was put back together by his devoted sister/wife. Physically resurrected for a night, Osiris fertilized the seed of eternity within the womb of Isis, who magically conceived a son named Horus. When he grew to manhood, Horus eventually challenged and overthrew his uncle (and father's murderer) and regained the throne of Egypt. Osiris henceforth ruled the realm of the dead. Isis continued on, in her believers' hearts and minds, as the Great Goddess of fertility, healing, justice, and magic; and the reputation of her omnipotence spread from Philae and Memphis to Greece, Sicily, and Pompeii. Altars to this Mistress of Heaven and Almighty Lady of Wisdom have been discovered on the banks of the Danube and the Thames, and temples dedicated to her existed at one time on the hill of the Capitoline in Rome and at St.-Germain-des-Prés in Paris. Astonishingly, some five thousand years after the first recorded acknowledgment of her existence, the Mother of All and her brother/husband/consort are still being worshiped today in many countries of the world—and their story is still being told.

I have long wanted to explore this resonant love story concerned with

betrayal and loyalty, death and rebirth, forgetting and memory, evil and righ-
teousness, duty and compassion; the manifestation of the forces of nature; the
meaning of sisterhood and brotherhood and of motherhood/fatherhood/son-
hood; and the mysteries of the body, the soul, and the spirit. There are many
books, essays, and articles, both scholarly and popular, about Isis and Osiris,
but as far as I know there is not one that has sought to illuminate the story
from the perspective of people who are *today* worshiping, devoting themselves
to, and even, in one sense or another, embodying these gods and enacting in
their lives the principles the gods represent.

Speaking for contemporary secular or monotheistic humanity, André Mal-
raux has asked, "What did our successive interpretations of Horus and Osiris
matter? The gods have no meaning if Olympus no longer has one; Anubis the
embalmer had no meaning if the world of the dead no longer has one. Each
of the gods had belonged to the impenetrable world of Truth that men
adored. Egypt had called Osiris back to life through its prayers, and we called
him back through his form and his legend—through everything *except* prayer."

My book does not intend to try to prove, disprove, justify, or disqualify
any claims or theories held by the individuals I report on. Incredulous as I
may be at times, my personal sense of skepticism and animal faith has never
prevented me from believing, along with the poet Wallace Stevens, that "reality is an activity of the most august imagination," and that those who are
living in the realm of the gods—abiding *inside* the faith and calling Isis and
Osiris and Horus back through prayer—have uncustomary and revelatory
things to tell and remind us about the nature of the gods.

At Clonegal Castle in southeastern Ireland I visited with Olivia Robertson, archpriestess and hierophant and one of the founders of the Fellowship
of Isis; she, with her brother the Reverend Lawrence Durdin-Robertson and
visiting priests and priestesses of a worldwide organization that consists of
some eleven thousand members in more than sixty countries, brings the story
of Isis and Osiris to life in mystery plays that are performed in the castle's
basement temple. In Cairo, Egypt, I met secretly with Her Grace Sekhmet
Montu, the spiritual leader of the Ammonite Foundation, the Foundation of

Ammon-Ra, which claims to have been founded by the boy-king Tutankha-mon; and it was there that I met Neb Heru, the nine-year-old son of Sekhmet Montu and her husband, His Excellency Ptah Hotep, who, I was told, is the incarnation of the god-being Horus. In Edmonton, Canada, I spent time with Evangeline and Franklin Kane, two therapists who have developed and lead an Isis/Osiris workshop that "embodies the drama of the mythic Isian/Osi-rian family in its cyclic deaths and resurrections" with pageant, dance, mask-making, and a mock entombment ceremony. Finally, I conversed with Dr. James P. Allen and Dr. Robert S. Bianchi about what Egyptologists today know about the story of Isis and Osiris, and with Mark Hasselriis, an artist and teacher of the symbolic meaning of Egyptian art, about the way in which the Isian/Osirian family is connected to the chakras of the kundalini system of yoga.

The story of Isis and Osiris has been with us in one form or another for at least five thousand years. Its tenacity and memorability derive from its pas-sionate account of the love of two soul mates; of the betrayal, but not the extirpation, of that love; and of the longing and searching for and the reunit-ing of the body of the beloved. To bind or tie together is one of the aims of religion (from the Latin word *religio*). One re-*members* and re-*collects* in order to heal and in order never to forget. By remembering and recollecting the story of Isis and Osiris, we keep in our hearts a tale that expresses, in Joseph Camp-bell's words, "the immanence of divinity in the phenomenal forms of the universe."

THE STORY OF ISIS AND OSIRIS

Isis and Osiris. Mortuary Papyrus of Nestanebetishru. 21st Dynasty.

*T*he Egyptian gods Osiris and Isis were both brother and sister, husband and wife. Their mother was Nut, Goddess of the Sky; their father was Geb, God of the Earth; and it is said that the twin brother and sister were already in love with each other in the womb of their mother.

As king and queen of Egypt in the first age of the world, these two gods bestowed on humankind the gifts of civilization. Osiris taught his subjects how to cultivate wheat, barley, and corn, how to brew beer and tend the vines; he introduced writing and astronomy; and he trained the people to worship the gods, enact the rites, and follow the laws he gave them. Isis provided medicines of healing and magical incantations, invented the loom, encouraged music and dancing, and dispensed the justice of the heart. Compassionate teachers of humanity, Osiris and Isis were from the moment of their conception a couple whose love passed understanding.

> *On the leaves of stars lay the boy,*
> *the moon in silver peacefulness,*
> *and the sundial's eye*
> *turned and watched him.*
> > *From the desert blew the red wind,*
> > *the coast deserted of sails.*

> *And the sister quietly took from the sleeper*
> *his sex, and devoured it.*

She gave him her soft red heart
in trade, and lay it upon him.

 And the wound grew vividly in the dream . . .
 And the moon and sun changed places . . .
 And he ate her heart, and she ate his.

Later, Osiris civilized the entire world as he journeyed through it, winning over the inhabitants by means of song, poetry, and words of gentle persuasion. But Osiris' loutish, cantankerous brother Set, who, along with his sister Nephthys, was also the offspring of Nut and Geb, was envious of his more famous and beloved sibling. Moreover, one fateful dark night, Osiris had mistaken Nephthys for Isis; the child of that illicit union was the jackal-headed god Anubis, guide of the souls of the dead in the underworld.

Set planned his revenge. Secretly he measured the body of Osiris and ordered an exquisitely decorated sarcophagus to be made to his brother's measurements. When Osiris returned from one of his trips abroad, Set invited him to a banqueting hall where hundreds of people were feasting and celebrating, and at the climax of the party he generously proposed that whoever lay down in the chest and demonstrated that it fit him alone could keep it as a gift. Many tried, to no avail; but when Osiris got in and lay down, seventy-two of Set's accomplices rushed into the room, slammed on the lid, secured it with bolts, sealed it with molten lead, carried it to the Nile, and tossed it in. Swept to the sea, the wooden sarcophagus drifted to the coast of Lebanon and was washed ashore at Byblos, where it came to rest in the branches of a sapling tamarisk tree. (See Illustration 2.1.) As the tree grew, it enclosed the chest in its trunk. So large, beautiful, and fragrant did this tree become that the king of Byblos noticed it one day

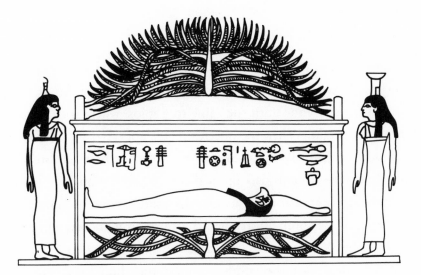

2.1: Osiris in the tamarisk tree. 1st century B.C. Dendera.

and ordered that it be cut down and used as a pillar to support the roof of his palace.

Isis, meanwhile, cut off one of her locks, put on mourning garments, and set out, grieving, to search for her beloved husband. She accosted strangers for information. Even when she encountered children, she asked them about the chest, for it was said that children had the power of divination, and people would take omens from children's shouts as they played near the temples.

A whistle or a cry,
Or let the game die!

Bushel of wheat,
Bushel of clover,
All not hid
Can't hide over!

Green man, arise!
Green man, arise!

Some children playing on the shore told her of a beautiful chest they had seen being carried eastward on the waves. So Isis followed the shoreline until she came to Byblos, where she sat down near a fountain. When the queen's maids appeared with their water pitchers, she greeted them and plaited their hair and breathed the fragrance of ambrosia upon them. When the queen observed her strangely transformed maids, she asked about the marvelous woman of the fountain, requested a meeting with her, and made Isis the nurse of her newborn prince.

It is said that the goddess nursed the child by putting her finger instead of her breast in his mouth; but at night she burned the mortal parts of his body, while she became a swallow flying around the pillar, making lament. One evening the queen came upon this scene and gave a shriek when she saw her child on fire. "I was burning away the mortal parts of your child so that he might live forever," Isis said, revealing herself to the queen. "Now, however, you have broken the spell, and he will die as all men must die." The king of Byblos asked the goddess to forgive his wife, and she agreed on the condition that she be given the tamarisk pillar under the castle roof. Then Isis cut open the pillar, drew forth the chest, and threw herself upon it and lamented.

Eventually, the chest was transferred to a royal barge. (See Illustration 2.2.) Isis set sail with it back home, and at the first opportunity during the voyage she removed the lid of the sarcophagus. Full of grief and heartbreak, she lay face-to-face on the body of her dead husband and held an inner dialogue with him.

And she saw the ghost of the death in him . . . and suddenly she was terrified, and she felt robbed. She felt the shadow of the gray, grisly wing of death triumphant.

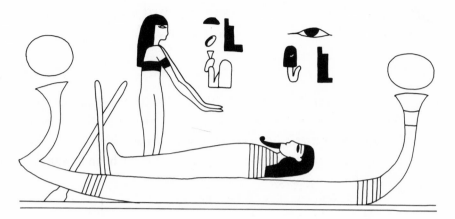

2.2: Isis with the recovered mummy of Osiris. 3rd–1st century B.C. Probably Philae.

"Ah, Goddess," he said. . . . "I would be so glad to live if you would give me my clue again."

For here again he felt desperate, faced by the demand of life, and burdened still by his death.

"Let me anoint you!" the woman said to him softly. "Let me anoint the scars! Show me, and let me anoint them!"

Having chafed all his lower body with oil, suddenly she put her breast against the wound in his left side, and her arms round him, folding over the wound in his right side, and she pressed him to her, in a power of living warmth, like the folds of a river. And the wailing died out altogether, and there was a stillness, and darkness in his soul, unbroken dark stillness, wholeness.

Then slowly, slowly, in the perfect darkness of his inner man, he felt the stir of something coming. A dawn, a new sun. A new sun was coming up in him, in the perfect inner darkness of himself. He waited for it breathless, quivering with a fearful hope . . . "Now I am not myself. I am something new. . . ."

It is said that one night Isis transformed herself into a falcon, with light emanating from her feathers and air from her wings, and by this means enabled Osiris' sex to rise from his inert body.

Drawing his essence from him, she conceived a child, Horus, his son, heir, and avenger. (See Illustration 2.3.) Then Osiris appeared to her in a dream.

He was standing under the trees, when the morning sun was hot, and the pines smelled sweet, and on the hills the last pear-bloom was scattering. She came slowly toward him, and in her gentle lingering, her tender hanging back from him, he knew a change in her.

"Hast thou conceived?" he asked her.

"Why?" she said.

"Thou art like a tree whose green leaves follow the blossom, full of sap. And there is a withdrawing about thee."

"It is so," she said. "I am with young by thee. Is it good?"

"Yea!" he said. "How should it not be good?"

She looked at him, and the peace of her maternity was troubled by anxiety.

"Let not your heart be troubled," he said. "I have died the death once."

So he knew the time was come again for him to depart. He would go alone, with his destiny. Yet not alone, for the touch would be upon him, even as he left his touch on her. And invisible suns would go with him.

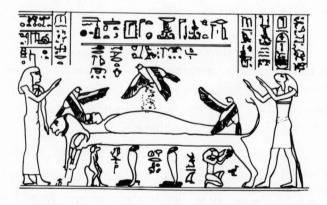

2.3: The fecundation of Isis-as-falcon. Abydos.

Isis arrived in Egypt and immediately went into hiding with her son. Constantly alert to the always-present danger of Set and his followers, the goddess raised Horus in the papyrus thickets, marshes, and swamps of the Delta, nursing and watching over him. (See Illustration 2.4.)

Horus speaks:

I am life rushing on, born from the egg of the world, from the belly of a magic woman, born of my father's dreams. I am the screech of wind, the rush of falcon wings, talons sharp as knives. I came after you. I stand before you. I am with you always. I am the power that dispels darkness. Look upon the dark face of my father

2.4: Isis in the papyrus swamps. 3rd–1st century B.C. Philae.

Osiris. He is nothing. Embrace him. Even nothing cannot last. The seed laid into the void must grow. The candle's only purpose is to shine in the darkness. Bread is meant to be ground to pulp in the teeth. The function of life is to have something to offer death. Ah, but the spirit lies always between, coming and going in and out of heaven, filling and leaving the houses of earth. A man forgets, but his heart remembers—the love and the terror, the weeping, the beating of wings.

And it came to pass that one night when the moon was full, Set and his entourage, out hunting, pursued a wild boar into the Delta swamps and came upon the body of Osiris. In a rage, Set cut his dead brother's body into fourteen pieces, one for each night of the waning moon, and then scattered them far and wide throughout the land of Egypt.

Once again Isis set out to search for her husband, this time accompanied by her sister Nephthys. They traveled the whole of the country, from the Delta to Nubia, re-membering Osiris, as they remembered him in their hearts, for to remember is to heal. Isis and Nephthys re-collected each member of their brother's body—head, heart, backbone . . . all except the phallus, which had been swallowed by a fish in the Nile—and they proceeded to reassemble the god. (See Illustration 2.5.) Then Anubis bent over his reunited father, placed him on a lion-headed bier, swathed him

2.5: Isis and Nephthys reconstituting the body of Osiris. Philae.

in linen bandages, and embalmed him. Thus it is said that Osiris was the first mummy. (See Illustration 2.6.)

Horus, meanwhile, had grown into a mettlesome young man and was now anxious to engage in combat with his usurping uncle Set in order to claim his stolen inheritance and avenge his father's death. Over a period of several days, the two rivals for the throne of Egypt fought a series of ferocious battles.

> Now Horus and Set came into reach. When each slammed a sword against the other's blade, the advantage was to Horus. His arms were stronger—that was clear from the shock to both—and His hands were fast. The smell of Set grew rank with the sweat of twice-fortified wine. Aware that the power He took from His grapes might soon evaporate, He went on attack, looking to confuse Horus with rapid moves from side to side, but His attack was

2.6: *The embalming of Osiris. The mummy lies on the lion couch with four jars of unguent beneath it. Anubis in the role of embalming wizard-priest bends over the deceased. Right and left are, respectively, Nephthys and Isis with their hands placed on* shen *signs symbolizing the solar circuit from day to night and renascent day.* 1090–945 B.C. 21st Dynasty. Papyrus of Khonsu-mes.

soon worn out by these exertions. Set drew back a step. Each tried to stir, each man searched for breath. Each was wondering whether the other was as quickly used-up as Himself. Now, They continued by the quiver of an elbow, or the inclination of a knee, just out of distance of each other. . . .

"Look upon the future God of the Living," cried Set and threw a handful of mud into Horus' face. Blinded, Horus in a vertigo of elbows and knees went tumbling over a stump into the swamp water. Immediately, Set pushed Horus' head and shoulders into the muck. Now, the boy's arms had to be used to keep His nose above the water. His weak legs were up behind Him on the stump. Down between His buttocks rammed the hard phallus of Set. . . . A scream went up from Horus like the wail of a mortal boy, while Set was throbbing with pride. . . .

Horus still owned the old thumb of Set that Isis tied into the thick hair of His head. Now, head down, the bolt of Set riding on His sphincter, He knew that if He did not escape, the Land of the Dead might yet be carved out of His bowels. So, He reached up a hand, tore out a gout of hair to free the thumb, and waved it in the air. Set's erection was lost.

Back and forth the battle turned, but eventually Horus, who had lost his left eye in the struggle, overcame Set. Finally he presented his uncle, tied and bound, to his mother; but Isis felt sudden remorse for her brother and set him free. Furious, Horus took his axe and cut off his mother's head, which was immediately, magically, and temporarily replaced with the head of the cow-goddess, Hathor.

Horus was surrounded by a field of lotus. It had flowered out of the first lotus that grew from His eyes, and a gazelle was feeding on the leaves. Isis, without hesitation, took milk from His gazelle. The animal never retreated as the Goddess approached for Isis was in the head of Hathor, and when did a gazelle have fear of a cow? Indeed, the animal barely knew she was being milked. She assumed this strange cow merely wished to pay homage and did not know, poor cow, how to begin. Now, discovering that nothing was desired of her but milk, the gazelle (none so secretly vain as the gazelle) stamped her front paws on Hathor's breast, then, in a panic at her daring, rushed off. Hathor went up to Horus, and licked His face, washing gazelle's milk over those outraged sockets where His vision had been. Delicately, She uncovered His loincloth so that the breeze which rose from the spring might soothe His parts, even as the milk gave balm to His empty sockets, and indeed this tender wind on His loins offered peace to the harsh blood-crusted void above His nose. Horus, receiving these caresses, felt seeds beginning to germinate where once His eyes had been. He wondered if flowers could grow from His brow, and reached up to touch the petals, but instead—through a waterfall of blood and tears and pearly milk—saw His own two hands, and cried aloud, "My mother has forgiven Me." In the next instant, He saw the sad, luminous eyes of Hathor, and smelled Her great tongue with its odor of earth and grass licking at His brows. Then He could only say, "How can I forgive Myself?"

She put a finger on His brow to convey the answer: Whatever He prized most had to be offered to His father. And Horus wondered what He could give up.

Even as He asked Himself, He looked out on the desert and it was uncommonly beautiful. The rocks were the color of rose, and the sands a powder of gold. Wherever light gleamed on stone, He saw gems. Beholding a vision of such generosity, Horus no longer debated. "O Father," He said, and His desire was to utter each word with dignity, "I, Horus, Your Son, have been returned My eyes in order that I may offer them to You."

It is said that the bestowal of the sacrificed Eye of Horus to the mummy of Osiris restored that god to life—an eternal life. And from then on, as King of the Underworld, Osiris held out the promise of eternal life and resurrection to all of his worshipers. (See Illustrations 2.7 and 2.8.)

For her part, Isis—Mistress of the Cosmos, Sovereign of All That Is Miraculous, Almighty Lady of Wisdom—became a uni-

2.7: *Osiris, Judge of the Dead.* 1317–1301 B.C. Hunefer Papyrus.

versal goddess. Her cult spread from Egypt to Asia Minor; from Cyprus, Crete, and mainland Greece to Sicily and Rome, whose empire took her as far north as Saint-Germain in Paris and the banks of the River Thames. The image of Isis nursing her child-savior would be taken over by the Christian Madonna, who also adopted the titles of the goddess—Sedes Sapiente (Seat of Wisdom), Regina Coeli (Queen of Heaven), Stella Maris (Star of the Sea). But it was in the Eternal City during the first century B.C. that Isis truly attained the apogee of her influence and glory. (See Illustration 2.9.)

> Brilliant from the sea, She rose, flower garlands crowning Her abundant hair that fell upon Her perfect neck. Set upon Her forehead was the circlet of mirror, attended by a serpent on each side, as the sheaves of wheat that rose from the circle shone in the moonlight. Her cape as dark as the night gathered in folds beneath Her left arm, flowing over the shoulder of Her right, all but covering the linen that lay white upon Her golden body, the weave of finest linen adorned by the crocus of yellow, the rose of red and the flame of brightest orange. Stars glittered along the edges of the blackness of the cape; stars circled on the cape of night around a

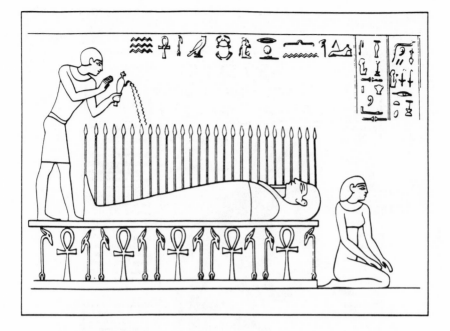

2.8: The drawing of Osiris with twenty-eight stalks of wheat growing out of his coffin ("The Resurrection of the Wheat") that deeply influenced the poet Walt Whitman:

> *Scented herbage of my breast,*
> *Leaves from you I glean, I write . . . ,*
> *Tomb-leaves, body-leaves growing up above me above death,*
> *. . . O the winter shall not freeze you delicate leaves,*
> *Every year shall you bloom again, out from where you retired you shall*
>   *emerge again . . .*

(Leaves of Grass)

mid-month moon. And upon the lowest hem that fell upon Her perfect ankles, the ripest fruits and the brightest of flowers wreathed in abundant border.

Encircled by the fingers of Her right hand was the sistrum rattle adorned with the face of the mighty Hathor, its thin copper discs moving along upon narrow rods in bell-like tones. Encircled in the fingers of Her left hand was the golden cup that formed the

2.9: *A woodblock of Isis—Queen of the Firmament, Star of the Sea, Nurturer of the World—by Athanasius Kircher (1601–1680), based on Apuleius' description of the goddess in* The Golden Ass

boat, its handle rising as uraeus cobra leading the fore. Her palm sandalled feet were scented with the finest incense and spices of Arabia, as Her voice resonated with these words:

I am Nature, Mother of All,
Ruler of the Elements, Progenitor of Worlds,
Chief of All Deities,
Mistress of the Living,
Mistress of the Dead,
The Sole Manifestation
of all goddesses and gods.
It is my will that controls
the planets of the sky,
the helpful winds of the sea,
and the grievous silence of the dead.
Though revealed by diverse customs and rites,
and called upon by many names,
my omnipotence is respected throughout the world.

To the Phrygians of Pessinus,
I am Mother of All Deities.
To the Athenians,
I am the wise and valiant Athena.
To those of the Cyprian Isle,
I am Aphrodite or Venus,
born of the foam of the Paphian coast.
To those of Crete who use the bow,
I am Dyktynna, Artemis, or Diana.

To those of the island of Sicily,
I am called Persephone or Proserpina.
To the Eleusinians,
I am Mother Demeter, Mother Ceres,
or simply Mother of Wheat.
Some call upon me as Hera or Juno,
Bellona or Hecate.
But both of the Ethiopian peoples,

those who live in Egypt
and those who dwell further to the East,
understand my ancient wisdom
more than any others,
for they know the ceremonies that are dear to me
and call me by my true name—
Almighty Isis.

Upon seeing Her perfect image, upon hearing Her perfect voice, Lucius Apuleius began to pray: "O Holy Blessed Lady, constant comfort to humankind whose beneficence and kindness nourish us all, and whose care for those in trouble is as a loving mother who cares for all her children—you are there when we call, stretching out your hand to put aside that which is harmful to us, untangling the web of fate in which we may be caught, even stopping the stars if they form a harmful pattern. All other deities, whether bountiful or merciless, do reverence to Thee. It is Isis who rules the world, stamping out the powers of evil, arranging the stars to give us answers, causing the seasons to come and go, commanding the winds to move ships, giving the clouds to water the growing seeds so that we may have food. If I had one thousand mouths and one thousand tongues within each, still I could not do justice to your Majesty. Yet I will forever remember your help in my time of need and keep your blessed image deep within my heart."

[*Note:* This retelling of the story of Isis and Osiris is based mainly on the famous version by Plutarch, written in Greek in the first century A.D. (*Of Isis and Osiris*), and also draws on some earlier Egyptian variants of the tale. I am indebted to the translations and paraphrases of Plutarch by Joseph Campbell, T. G. H. James, Eberhard Otto, and Barbara Watterson. I have interspersed the narrative with excerpts from several modern versions of the story: part of the lyric poem "Isis und Osiris," written in 1923 by the Austrian writer Robert Musil (translated by Manuela Wacha and Jonathan Cott), which sees the goddess-and-god as a hermaphroditic couple; *The Man Who Died* by D. H. Lawrence, which recounts the story of an unresurrected Christ who is born again as Osiris in the arms of a priestess of Isis; *Awakening Osiris: A Translation of the Egyptian Book of the Dead* by Normandi Ellis; and *Ancient Evenings* by Norman Mailer, which contains the most volatile and audacious version of the Isis and Osiris story of recent times. The concluding paean to the goddess appears in *The Golden Ass* by the second-century Latin writer Lucius Apuleius (in the translation of William Adlington), which describes how the author, trapped in the body of a donkey, is finally restored to human form with the aid of the Goddess Isis. The children's rhymes are taken from *Children's Games in Street and Playground* by Iona and Peter Opie.]

3

ISIS AND OSIRIS:

A Conversation with

James P. Allen

*D*r. James P. Allen is the former head of the American Research Center in Egypt, the author of *Genesis in Egypt: The Philosophy of Ancient Egyptian Creation Accounts*, and currently an associate curator of the Department of Egyptian Art at the Metropolitan Museum of Art in New York City. The following conversation took place in Dr. Allen's spacious office—as quiet as a tomb—just off a corridor of the museum's Temple of Dendur gallery. Surrounded by scores of reference books, figurines and artifacts (both old and modern), and a hieratic desktop computer, he and I talked for two hours about Isis and Osiris in this inner sanctum of the Metropolitan's great collection of the Egyptian past:

The myth of Isis and Osiris that we get as a whole in Plutarch (*Of Isis and Osiris*, A.D. 120) is nowhere spelled out in full in the ancient Egyptian sources. It probably existed as an entire story in pretty much the same way it shows up in Plutarch, but we don't have that. There are *references* to it, however, and knowing the whole story allows us to give a context to the pieces. The Pyramid Texts are the earliest coherent religious texts we know of (Fifth Dynasty, c. 2500–2400 B.C.), and there are already mentions of Isis and Osiris in these that are close to what we read of them in Plutarch. Then there are "The Songs of Isis and Nephthys" (fourth century B.C.); the texts from the temples of Edfu, Dendera, and Philae; and *The Contendings of Horus and Set*, from the New Kingdom. And there are others. When you come down to it, they're all about the eternal mystery of life and death—where life comes from and what happens when you die, the hope for life after death. It's pretty basic stuff, and it exists in one form or another in almost every religion in the world.

The Osiris part is actually easier to understand than the Isis part. For the Egyptians, the gods were principles of nature (we'd call them physical principles)—other beings who were different from them. The principle that makes life come from apparent death was called Osiris. You could see it in a number of manifestations. Place an apparently dead seed on the ground and a little later, by some miracle, a live plant is produced. Obviously, the plant wasn't inside that little seed; something must have acted to make that happen—and that something was Osiris. You could see it in the inundation that spread over the land, apparently destroying it, and then receded and produced life—*that* was Osiris. And, primarily for the Egyptians, you could see it every day in the life and death of the sun. The sun went down, and the people didn't know where it went; they weren't certain that it was going to rise in the morning. Each dawn was a new miracle. And what happened was that the sun united with the principle of rebirth, which was Osiris in the netherworld, and came up again.

There are many theories about what the name Osiris really means. The best guess is that it means something like "the Seat of the Eye," the eye being the sun and Osiris the place where the sun goes. Isis is Osiris' female counterpart; her name seems to mean "seat" or "place." Scholars have thought that Isis and Osiris were gods of kingship. Osiris was said to be the male ancestor of the king who conferred life on the *new* king, and Isis was the principle of legitimacy—the actual physical throne that the king sat on. But it seems to me that just as Osiris is the male principle, Isis is the female principle—and these have to combine in order to make life possible. Which is why Isis, as the female counterpart of Osiris, is also called his sister.

Now, as Isis is the female counterpart of Osiris, Set is the antithesis of Osiris. Osiris represents the ordered, controlled principle of life, which you find in cultivation, for example; Set is the wild—but not evil—uncontrolled, lusty aspect of life.

Osiris is the cultivated land, Set is the desert. But the desert is also good because it protects Egypt from its enemies. There are pictures in papyri that show Set standing at the prow of the sun boat, guarding it as it passes through the dangers of the night.

But sometimes chaos gets out of control, as it does in real life, and it overcomes the principles of harmonious existence, which are Osiris. Then wrong and disorder reign. But out of all this, order returns—something that is explained in the Isis and Osiris myth when the dead Osiris is re-membered by Isis, who conceives Horus from him. Horus grows up and eventually conquers chaos—Set—and imposes order once again.

When Set and Horus are battling each other, they are said to sodomize each other. This is actually depicted not only in *The Contendings of Horus and Set* but also, as we have known since 1977, in the Pyramid Texts themselves. In Pyramid Text 501C, for example, which was found on the antechamber east wall of the Pyramid of Pepi I in Saqqara, we read, "Horus screeched [made a sound like a heron or benben bird] on account of his eye . . . broken . . . and Set yelled [made another sound of a bird] because his testicles were cut off. [This castration means that 'uncontrolled chaos' has been 'controlled.'] Horus has conducted his semen into Set's anus; Set has conducted his semen into Horus' anus." I should tell you that this passage appears in a spell against snakes, and serves as the mythological precedent cited at the beginning of the spell to give validity to what follows.

But remember, you can't take the actions and events in the story literally. From what we know today, sodomy was probably unacceptable to the ancient Egyptians. One of the Negative Confessions in the *Book of the Dead*, for instance, states that "I have not had relations with a male wife." The point of the translation I read to you has to do with *two principles uniting*. To the Egyptians, the conquest and the annihilation of something was never the goal. Rather, it was the incorporation, the peaceful coexistence of things, that was important. It's a way of describing how the chaotic force, Set, and the ordered force,

Osiris, could find accord in one principle—which was, of course, the king, Horus.

Now, in a sense, that fragment from the Pyramid Texts is like the ancient Egyptian story of how the universe came about. First there was a single god named Atum (which means "monad"), who produced everything. For the Egyptians, creation was procreation. But if you were alone, there was nothing to procreate *with*. So they had Atum masturbating; and his first children were the result of that action. It doesn't mean that the Egyptians literally thought that there was once a god who masturbated and created the world. Rather, it was a way of trying to explain how, materially and causally, everything could come from one source, how you could get multiplicity from unity. Like our big bang. It's another explanation of the same thing.

It might be said that the Egyptian gods are very close to what we today would consider scientific theories that are continually refined, the way Newtonian physics moves toward quantum physics. We've separated our understanding of the universe from religion, but to the ancient Egyptians they were one and the same thing. We speak of the four force fields of the universe—the weak force, the strong force, gravity, and electromagnetism. The Egyptians came up with nine (the Ennead, a group of nine gods) or ten (if you want to include Horus). (See Illustration 3.1.)

It goes like this. First there's Atum, who produces Shu and Tefnut; both mean "atmosphere." You see, the ancient Egyptian concept of the world is like a box. The sky is the skin of the infinite ocean, and the earth lies in the middle. What keeps the ocean off the earth is the upper atmosphere, called Shu, and the atmosphere underneath the earth, called Tefnut. So the first thing Atum creates is a kind of bubble in what is otherwise an infinite ocean of water. We think of it as a vacuum, but the Egyptians thought of it as water.

So the seed out of which everything originated is Atum. And just as the plant is somehow in the seed, even though it's entirely different, so everything that follows is Atum, too.

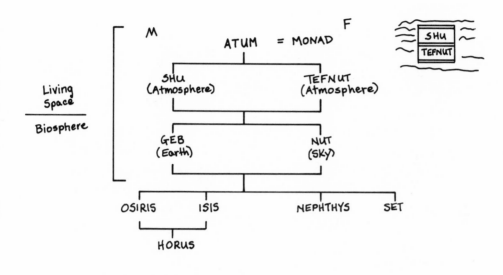

3.1.

Atum "develops" into Shu and Tefnut . . . and so on. In one papyrus, Atum says, "After I developed, development developed." That's really a sophisticated thought, and the ancient Egyptians could and did think in that way.

From the existence of Shu and Tefnut came Geb (Earth) and Nut (Sky), and it's the existence of the atmosphere that distinguishes between the two—these two children who are dependent on the atmosphere. What this means is that the first process of creation has produced biosphere—the space in which life can take place. Once that has come into existence, then the principle of life is possible, which is Isis and Osiris and Set and Nephthys. So the physical universe, the arena of male and female, life and death, makes possible the *spiritual* universe—the immaterial processes of life, like the idea of rebirth embodied by Osiris.

The story of Isis and Osiris is the closest thing to a popular religion that ancient Egypt had. Every family *was* Isis and Osiris and Nephthys and Set and Horus, because the family con-

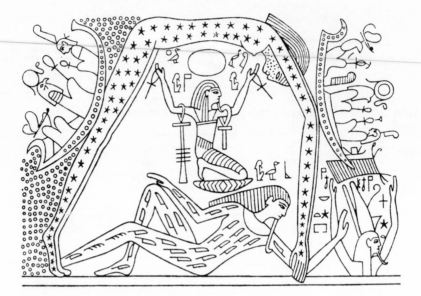

3.2: Shu separates the sky and the earth (shown in the form of Geb and Nut). Mythological mortuary papyrus of Tentamun. 21st Dynasty.

sisted of mother and father and sister and brother and child. It's the continuing story of life. And as we've said, the gods are still with us. We just call them different things. Those who worship Isis and Osiris have simply singled out one aspect to identify with—though to me, it's the same as worshiping electromagnetism or gravity. On the other hand, without them, we wouldn't be around!

But to follow the ancient Egyptian way of thinking: even the four force fields that modern science has identified (and perhaps a fifth, if there is a fifth) would, they would have said, have to be subordinate, since they all came from *somewhere*. The ultimate thing is God. And the Egyptians reasoned back to that, too. They reasoned back to an ultimate principle, which was not Atum. Because if you have all matter in one point existing for all eternity in the primeval waters, why should it all of a sudden change? So what they posited was that you could explain creation not from within creation, only from outside it.

And that's what they called Amon, or Amun, which means "hidden." It's hidden because it's not part of creation, it's the *principle* that made all things. So you see, the Egyptians *reasoned* to monotheism. They didn't just say that Amon was the only god; this was the god who *created* the gods. And there were gods. And the Egyptians worshiped them.

It seems to me that those today who worship a goddess like Isis are actually worshiping the mother principle; those worshiping Osiris are worshiping the resurrection principle, and are in this process coloring the gods with their own perceptions. But even if this is the case, it all seems to be powerful and attractive to people, not only because of the mystery of it but also because it is all so ultimately basic.

You could do worse than Isis and Osiris.

4

THE FELLOWSHIP

OF ISIS AT

CLONEGAL CASTLE

Olivia Robertson and her brother Lawrence Durdin-Robertson in priestly attire at Brighid's Well in the Temple of Isis, Clonegal Castle, Ireland, 1987. Photograph by Jeremy Nicholl.

Friends, companions on the quest for eternal life, join us in the Temple of Isis at Clonegal Castle, that we may enact one of the most ancient mysteries of all time—the Mystery of the Awakening of Osiris by the Goddess Isis, his wife. You are in your time and space, and I am a voice from the future, in another time and space. I am Olivia Robertson of the Fellowship of Isis, and I offer to be your guide in a mystical journey to the land of Ireland.

It is late September 1990, and this afternoon Olivia Robertson, archpriestess and hierophant, is standing with eyes closed and arms raised in the drawing room of Clonegal Castle in misty County Carlow, Ireland, proclaiming and recording a spontaneous introduction to one of her Isian mystery plays. In one hand she holds the microphone of a cassette machine, and in the other she vigorously shakes a sistrum, the ancient Egyptian rattle sacred to the Goddess Isis. An hour ago, she officiated at the Rite for the Consecration of a Hierophant of Isis, initiating a young American woman who worships the Goddess in a small coastal town on the Florida panhandle and who traveled to Ireland especially for this occasion, which took place in the Temple of Isis in the cavernous basement of the castle. Now Olivia Robertson has reassembled in the drawing room the splendidly robed participants from that ceremony in order to begin recording a dramatized reading and enactment of the Mystery of the Awakening of Osiris, which will shortly continue in the temple. Tapes of this spiritual drama will then be made available to other members of the Fellowship of Isis, an organization of some eleven thousand people living in more than sixty countries, including Ireland, Japan, Nigeria, the United States, India, and New Zealand.

Olivia is wearing a black embroidered dress decorated with Isian emblems and is adorned with a symbolic gold girdle and topaz ring and a copper serpent-crown that rests on her thick, waist-length brown hair. She has placed a shoulder-high lotus wand against the wall. In her early seventies, with clear brown eyes and only a few wisps of gray to suggest her age, she has the air, manner, and theatrical aplomb of a fourteen-year-old Duse about to perform for invisible gods.

In the slightly faded grandeur of this room filled with Rosenthal teacups, Dresden china, a slightly cracked bowl from the Imperial Palace in Peking, a Vauxhall mirror, and an elegant chandelier, she turns on a tape recorder next to her recording cassette, and we now hear the soft, meditative strains of music for synthesizer, harp, and flute. Thinking of her distant audience, Olivia conjures up a Halloween Eve—though that is still a month away—as she raises her hands, shakes the sistrum, and, in a spellbound, incantatory voice, declaims to unseen listeners:

> You feel yourself now happy and joyful, comfortable in your own world, but you long for something greater that has been awaiting you all these years. . . . You are my future and I am your past. *Rise* from your body, *ascend* from where you are, and I want you to take a journey into the past, at Samhain [Halloween], the thirty-first of October, the beginning of the mysteries of Isis and Osiris, which were enacted at that time in the temples of Egypt with their mighty columns, their hieroglyphs speaking the mysteries. You can see a rainbow glow of etheric light about the castle. Now we descend, and we come across a woman veiled in black [Olivia Robertson herself]. And we see she is in deep trance, and we know that what is awaited is the oracle of the Goddess. The oracles ceased when Egypt fell to the Romans, but now they are returned. The priest-

hierophant of Osiris stands forth holding a great shepherd's crook. He invokes the divine Goddess, that She may speak to us once more.

While Olivia has been communing with and guiding her astral travelers, she has been joined in the drawing room by her brother, the Reverend Lawrence Durdin-Robertson, an ordained clergyman of the Anglican Church and the twenty-first baron of Strathloch, whom everyone calls Derry. It was on Saint Patrick's Day in 1966 that Derry had a sudden illumination on the castle grounds, "receiving," he recalls, "a powerful electric shock as the revelation that God was a woman was made to me—a sign, I learned later, that I was receiving power from the Goddess." He offered to the bishop of Ossory his resignation as a minister in the Church of Ireland, but the bishop refused to accept it, saying that the revelation didn't make much difference to Durdin-Robertson's vocation. In order to "bring parity," however, as Derry wished to do, between Jesus and the Goddess, he and his sister have since inexorably insisted on writing about the Goddess and Her attributes in capital letters ("Divine Isis, Goddess of Ten Thousand Names, I invoke Your Grace").

Tonight, this heteroclete minister, now also ordained as a priest of Isis, appears in his black poplin academic gown and hood, a black-and-blue crown of ancient Egypt on which are entwined two golden serpents, and a black-and-gold stole. Durdin-Robertson, who spends most of his time immersed in writing scholarly tomes on the Goddess, has descended from his upstairs library to join the ceremony. Suffering temporarily from severe laryngitis and an attack of rheumatism, he uses the shepherd's crook he is holding as a cane to take some hesitant, painful, but dignified steps toward his sister. Approaching her, he slowly, faintly, but clearly begins to utter an ancient invocation to Isis, the Goddess of Ten Thousand Names:

> Isis of the Thousand Names, Who protecteth the soul with Thy feathery wings of the kite, Whose blood, enchantments, and power strengthen the soul, inspire us with Breath of the West Wind. Winged Goddess, Who concealeth Thy brow with Thy long hair, spread Thy hair of enchantment and shake it over the brow of Thy devotees. Breathe into us Thy Breath of life and health and strength.

In a Garboesque voice, the priestess Olivia pronounces the oracle of the Goddess Isis:

> It is through Inspiration that you live. Without Inspiration you are as dead, devoid of the Holy Breath. Do not deceive yourselves. You cannot live forever shut in the mummy-cases of your own fantasies, however colorful they are, however compelling. For without Inspiration the colors will dim, the power lessen. No amount of stimulation from your thought or from your senses, no act of will, can then bring life. You will slowly sink into unconsciousness, and as your dreams become nightmares, you yourselves will fall victims to your self-created images of fear.
>
> Draw upon the Breath of Isis, which is wafted to you and all beings through the rhythmic beating of Her wings. This Holy Breath may not be concealed, conserved, kept imprisoned in one place, within one person—even within one God or Goddess. It is for all. And as it is for all, it brings all. Open yourselves to the wind of Inspiration, and you lose nothing but the hardening case of a coffin of outworn theologies and cramping laws. Instead, you will gain the riches of eternity and make better theologies, nobler laws. Allow Truth to cleanse your minds as a strong wind brings renewal. For Truth expresses herself as new understanding, and she may not be bound or blindfolded. This courage to face the unveiled Truth means that you lose the sleep of nonentity. You breathe freely, you open your eyes fearlessly: you sit; you stand;

then, with the wings of Horus, you fly with Me. You use the many-colored winding-sheet of dreams that once bound you as a robe that you wear at will.

Hear the call of Isis and awaken!

"My red-haired niece once said to me, 'I'm so furious at my Quaker cousin. She says I have to be dull and good like *her* and not wicked and interesting like Aunt Olivia!' Would you like a biscuit?"

I am having tea with Olivia, who is wearing a vermilion velvet jacket and a matching red scarf. It is the following afternoon, and we are in the conservatory, a large, airy room at the front of the castle which faces an expansive lawn and a long row of yew trees and is dominated by an immense, all-embracing vine—a cutting from the famous vine at Hampton Court, planted in Clonegal Castle around 1900. The vine bears purple grapes, and as Olivia offers me one ("Here, it's delicious!"), she declares, "It's *so* nice to realize that one is eating from the same fruit as did Anne Boleyn and Nell Gwyn!"

A thin, diminutive, high-spirited woman who could easily play the role of one of the witches in *The Wonderful Wizard of Oz* ("I'm not a witch, but I *am* psychic," she asserts), Olivia continually displays a sparrowlike quickness of gesture and speech, darting from one subject to another with surprising asides and startling non sequiturs ("Do you know if you feed bees sugar they get diarrhea?" she asked one journalist, apropos of nothing). She has a lively, witty, and eccentric sense of humor; believes in reincarnation, UFOs, and ghosts ("We prefer to think of them as 'spirit friends,'" she says); and intersperses her unflaggingly dramatic and rapid discourse with plummy public school locutions and exclamations like "Golly!" and "Gosh!" and "Absolutely smashing!" as if she were a character out of a children's book by Angela Brazil or Enid Blyton. "You see," Olivia explains, "if you think of your life as a circle, a great circuit, and not as a segment, you realize you need to *keep it all*. Most people do it in this linear way, one, two, three, four, hitting one note at a time each day. So when they're old, they've lost middle age, and when they're middle-aged, they've lost youth. What *we* do is go in a circle and play all the notes of the piano all the time. You want to play the symphony of life and not be stuck in one little bar of it."

But when asked a question that requires an extended answer, as when I inquire how she became what she is today, Olivia becomes silent, closes her eyes, and slowly replies. "If you could let me tune in a bit, because I'm rather inclined to talk inspirationally . . ." Then, after another long pause, she brings herself back to what her red-haired niece said about her.

"The Protestant church, in which I was brought up, used to suggest that if you wore makeup or looked glamorous or were an actress, you were 'bad.' So when my niece said what she did about me, I thought, 'Well, I've really made it!' Because I'm *totally* virgin, I never break the law, I'm very correct. And yet I have the great fun now of having been in the *News of the World* ["Goddess of Love Cult Shocks a Rural Eden"].

"I remember once seeing a 'bad' woman, a Guinness lady, and I got so excited. She had bright yellow hair hanging down, a black dress, a long string of pearls, and she was jolly and kicking around. She was labeled 'bad,' you see. Catherine of Russia was 'bad,' and Mrs. Simpson was 'bad' because she was divorced. I, however, thought they were *marvelous*. And I've always been attracted by actresses and the like . . . but they seemed to be *drunk* a lot of the time, and they smoked, they swore, and they appeared to be on a wrong footing. Not until later did I realize that they were using witchcraft power—scent, hand movements, the way they leaned forward to show their breasts—though they didn't *know* they were doing magic. I don't think witches existed when I was a girl. But I was certainly aware of this good/bad division.

"My brother was asked in the army, 'What's your sister Olivia like? Is she good, pretty, or clever?' And he said I was a bit of all three. You see, I produced 'normal' books at one time—I was an 'Anglo-Irish author'—and they always photographed me as though my hair were permanently waved, and with a cold, pure look. One of my books, a novel called *Field of the Stranger*, was even a Book Society choice. I was very pleased, and on that occasion I wanted to be photographed looking *romantic*. So I went to a place that had Dawn beauty products and said that I was an actress. And then they got out the chiaroscuro and showed my cheekbones. But if you were photographed for the *Irish Tatler and Sketch* or something, they'd take a *ghastly* photo of you intended to make you look suitable for marrying a gentleman, with your hair nice and parted, your face sort of fluffy and featuring a 'good' expression—dead like a fish—as if you'd been out riding the hounds, and wearing a pearl necklace, real pearls or nothing.

"Every family had its black sheep. Naturally, we had one—in this case, a male cousin who did three awful things: he became a Roman Catholic, he joined the Sinn Fein, and he was a homosexual! He was *completely* ostracized by his mother and clergyman father. But the butler felt sorry for him, secretly kept him in the butler's wing, and brought him up trays of food. He was thought of as a ghost, as if he had already died in the wilderness. While we—the good, the righteous—repudiated him.

"Just as my mother repudiated another of our relatives. The great poet Robert Graves was my second cousin. [Olivia's grandmother, Lady Parsons, was born Florence Graves.] Now, the Graves family was very spiritual but showed characteristics of *a bit of sex*, since many of the men seemed to have mistresses. I myself

longed to meet Robert Graves, but Mummy told me that although he was an extraordinary man, he lived on a barge with a
woman called Laura Riding, who kept trying to commit suicide.
And they wore sandals, which my mother disapproved of. You
weren't among the righteous if you wore sandals. They 'lived in
sin.' So as I couldn't meet *them*, I might meet the rather vulgar
journalist brother, Charles Graves, who actually was very nice. He
wasn't doing any sin, particularly. When Robert Graves received
a medal from your President Eisenhower, he was okay. But in my
day, he was *definitely* a sinner.

"Men sinners got away with it, if they were successful, but
women sinners were *finished*. A lady should only appear in the
newspaper when she was born, married, or died. So this was the
situation I was faced with. People who lived an instinctive life of
the old ways were ruled by their emotions and hence became the
unrighteous. If they turned to religion, it was of a hysterical fundamentalist kind, such that they kept shouting 'Alleluia!' which
was regarded by the upper class as *very bad form*. 'Emotion' was a
dirty word. Mummy used to say that if a man threw himself
howling on his wife's grave, it was *terrible*; one should *never* cry in
public.

"Americans were considered to be rather trashy and noisy.
England was still clutching on to Greece, but Hollywood was
Troy, was Carthage, was the old matriarchy jazzed up with vulgar
razzmatazz—all under Venus. And everything pertaining to Venus was vulgar! We didn't know whether Americans had emotions
or not. But *we* met the *right* sort of Americans, and they repudiated
the *wrong* sort. The best thing we could say about Americans was
that if they were like us, they were all right.

"There were mavericks around, however—dukes who drank,
swore, and were emotional. And I noticed in them one thing that
I wanted: they had *magic!* And I found I was alone in loving, ad-

miring, and being friends with people like that. Then I began reading about Nell Gwyn, Madame de Pompadour, and Catherine the Great, who also had something I couldn't quite put my finger on. And what they had was *also* magic. Some of that sort could even be saints—you had Mary Magdalene on one side, the Virgin Mary on the other. And there I was, a follower of Apollo in white, withdrawn, sitting in a corner, and taught that if I lost my virginity—unless, of course, I was married—I'd go forth among the sinners.

"Then in 1946 I had a mystical experience in which I transcended this duality and found the All God, including Goddess—everything! I was instructed that I was an intellectual snob, I was a humbug. And I thought I was dead, I couldn't go on living the way I had been. I found my teachers and they showed me an image of Christ as Dionysus. Actually, first they showed me Christ as Apollo surrounded by all the 'good' women in history. Then they showed me another picture of him as Dionysus with all the 'baddies.' And I began to wonder. Nell Gwyn had a heart of gold. Was she 'bad'? What is Christian, what is not? And everything began to come together.

"In the late 1960s I attended a lecture about witchcraft, and there was an empty seat behind me. And I became psychically aware of Mary Magdalene being there. She had very frizzy, orangey-colored hair, and she wasn't wearing all that Pre-Raphaelite stuff—rather a white-brushed dress, bunched in at the waist and patterned with white and red and black Arabic-type letters. She had a face like Vanessa Redgrave's, keenly intelligent, with a strong chin, straight brow. And she was leaning forward, saying, 'This is the way it was, this is the way it was.' Of *course!* She had been possessed by seven spirits. Do you remember? Jesus cast the spirits out, he probably wanted her to be in control of herself. And when Judas said, 'Do you know what manner of woman this is?' he meant something much worse than a prostitute. She was what we would later call a witch, with those occult powers. And I thought, 'Yes, these things are beginning to fall into place.' "

One of four children (a now-deceased sister, Barbara, and two brothers, Lawrence and Esmond), Olivia Robertson was born in London in 1917 to a family of soldiers, clergymen, politicians, and colonial administrators. Her father, Manning, of Scots-Irish ancestry, was a renowned town planner and architect. Her mother, Nora, an Anglo-Irish aristocrat, shot crocodiles as a girl in India, was the author of several noted books on salmon fishing, was reputed to be the number-one angler in Ireland, and invented the fly known as the Black Maria.

During World War I, the Durdin-Robertsons evacuated to Cirencester. It was there, when she was three months old, that Olivia recalls "coming to total consciousness. I became aware that I'd been in a very deep sleep—I saw the back of a red-brick house, I was in a pram facing it—and I absolutely *came to*, became myself . . . I knew I was *me*, I was absolutely collected. And then I went to sleep again. My mother called it 'Olivia's little glimpse.' Much later on, I described the house and the garden to her, and she told me it was Cirencester I was talking about. I'd only been there when I was an infant. And as an infant I had *known* that I was a baby and that I'd incarnated and that I would have to have a long, long sleep. . . . And then life was all the more ordinary again."

When she was five, Olivia moved with her family to Reigate, in Surrey ("a suburban, well-off place"), and she eventually attended Heathfield School in Ascot. "I was what people call clever," Olivia states, "a strong, right-hand brain person, a totally orthodox Christian, a pacifist, a liberal who didn't believe in the supernatural much. I think that if you want to conceal anything, talk. So I was a great talker. On the other hand, I went to see *La Traviata* and cried. My mother said, 'Hard, clever little Olivia, how *could* you cry at that rot?' And I used to listen to Beethoven's late quartets and daydream and take a little astral trip, but Daddy only saw that I was being highbrow and praised me for that. But all along, there was the *secret starry self* that loved magic."

At eight, Olivia first visited her family's fifty-room castle in southeastern Ireland, which had been occupied by the IRA and the Free State forces from 1916 to 1923. First built in 1625, Clonegal Castle (or Huntington Castle, as it was also known) had kept its crenelated, semicircular tower and its seventeen-foot well dating from pre-Christian times, which made Olivia feel as if she were the conservator of the Well at the World's End, with its Water of Life. And in her castle, situated between the Slaney and Derry rivers, amid green fields and soft brown hills, she dreamed that the original hall fireplace was actually a doorway leading to other, invisible wings and rooms with different furnishings and inhabitants—an extension to other worlds.

But even the everyday castle and its grounds were enchanted enough, with the six-hundred-year-old Yew Walk, a line of 120 trees bending over like wizened spirits to form an arch, under which ghostly hooded monks were said to walk after dark; the ruins to the north of the castle, known as the Abbey, which may originally have been used by monks or anchorites; the Front Avenue, consisting of majestic lime trees planted in the 1680s, which rose as high as 110 feet and provided an imposing grand entrance to the castle from the village; the Bullawn Stone, thirty yards southeast of the Front Avenue—a huge granite boulder with a cup-shaped hollow on top that, when filled with rainwater, was, and still is, said to cure warts. In the dank, mysterious castle itself, Olivia explored a maze of tenebrous and musty oak-paneled corridors with thick, damp woolen carpets; stared at the suit of chain mail, ceremonial halberds, and buffalo heads decorating the walls; sat with a candle in the basement dungeon with its six-foot-thick walls, where the IRA had not long before incarcerated prisoners; and, in almost every room, stared at the tapestries and portraits of her ancestors in old gilded frames.

"Lord Esmonde, a Protestant nobleman," Olivia explains, "started building the castle in 1625. His first wife was Ellice [Eilis] O'Flaherty, granddaughter of Grace O'Malley [Grainne Mhaoil], the hereditary queen of Connaught and rival of Queen Elizabeth. Legend has it that she haunts the Spy Bush, a holly bush at the foot of our Back Avenue. She combs her hair in the moonlight, accompanied by a white cat with green eyes.

"Two other ghosts—'spirit friends,' I prefer to say—are Barbara St. Leger, of Lord Doneraille's family—she sat for a portrait in a white fichu and a blue gown—and her lady's maid, Honor Byrne. Barbara married my ancestor Alexander Durdin in the late eighteenth century. She is said to walk up and down the chapel passage at night, keys jangling at her skirt. Honor Byrne also frequents the passage, and wipes down the door with her hair—exactly why, I don't know."

After her public school days, Olivia studied art at the Royal Hibernian Academy in Dublin, exhibited her paintings in that city when she was twenty-one, and wrote five novels and a book entitled *St. Malachy's Court*, which described the activities of Dublin slum children at eight playgrounds where Olivia had served for four and a half years as a play leader. She illustrated this book with her own sketches of the children. "Down at a playground one day," she remembers, "suddenly it came to me: why was I, like everyone else—including the supervisors—clock-watching, waiting till I could get off? *This* was eternal, *now*, these *children*. And I thought, I can never now be a mother, my heart has gone out to all of them, all those tinker children—the Ratchfords, the mad Murphys. Many of them had ringworm, lice, consumption, and were undernourished, but their joy in life was strong. And I thought, I'm going to live forever *now*, not think about meeting Prince Charming or going to smart parties or whatever. I was perfectly happy there.

"Now, my personality change took a very long time," Olivia explains to me. "I was a successful linear-logical, intellectual author. But after I had this inner merging of the outer and the inner, the left and the right, the high and the low, I found that I couldn't work, because I was too embarrassed to write about anything spiritual; I thought people would laugh at me. All I wanted to do was to read. I wanted to be entirely by myself. So I moved into a flat in our family home in Dublin. I read the ancient Greek dramas and fairy tales and mythology. I read every book I could find on every religion. And so far from finding the true one, I found that they were *all* true.

"This went on from 1946 to the late 1950s. My brother Derry, who worked as a clergyman in Wicklow and Norfolk, began to get mystical. And then, at last, in 1963 I met people like myself, and we started a semiprivate Center for Meditation and Study here at Clonegal Castle, where we did deep occult work—clairvoyance, mediumship, trance-inducing—and shared the same guides. I myself joined spiritualist associations, the Theosophists, a World Healing group. I celebrated Christmas, I went to Alice Bailey's groups, I visited clairvoyants. Then people discovered that I offered healing. And I found that when I did so, the clients went into trance. I touched someone, and off they'd go. But eventually I realized that I didn't like being a hypnotist, it was too strong. I preferred healing in different ways. The only thing I gave up was exclusiveness. I remember someone saying to me at that time, 'Oh, you're a seeker.' And I replied, 'No, I'm a finder.'"

But there was someone whom Olivia couldn't find—someone

she has hinted she knew in previous incarnations. "I've had the experience," Olivia confides in me, "of seeing my *own* twin soul as a god, as a beam of light. Then why did I want to have my own *human being* sitting with me and eating cornflakes or whatever for breakfast? But I did. Why, when I had seen the God, as it were—my own Osiris rising—did I want to go wandering around London, seeking, when I had *seen* him? It was that I wanted the human being.

"The funny thing is that I'd been told who he was and had been, and who *I* had been, in a previous life—all of *that* is private—but I went on and on searching, from 1946 to 1974, in London, in Paris . . . not in Dublin, I knew he'd never been there. But I thought he might be alive *now*, physically. I thought he liked classical music, so I went to the Albert Hall and looked around— I used to pretend that I was looking for a friend, thinking of that passage from the *Song of Songs*: 'I charge you, O daughters of Jerusalem, if ye find my beloved . . .'

"Now, one of the commands I'd been given stated that he and I were *not* to meet, it should not be . . . and that I had to accept that—I could never force or challenge the issue. But in spite of this, I'd be thinking that I'd try crying and that the person would come through to me in a dream. Or I'd say, 'I'm in trouble, please help.' But I realized I mustn't do that. It was like Pamina and Tamino in *The Magic Flute*—we each had to do our separate work.

"Finally, I went to a certain place in London, where I discovered his grave—he'd been a man of the Victorian age. I looked at it and said, 'That is dead.' I'd found the body of Osiris—there it was! And when I got back to Ireland, I told myself that I was not going to wander around searching anymore. I decided to stop *haunting* places.

"Therefore, I can see how Isis saw Osiris as a god. She wanted to marry him, as I did, and have breakfast and argue! And I felt that the man *I* had wanted also wished to marry a woman, *not* a goddess. But it's very odd when you've seen that which is perfect and heavenly and still desire someone who misplaces one of his shoes and brushes his teeth and is a human being.

"I was the intellectual type, the cold, Dianic, friendship type, while my twin soul was like Dionysus—very passionate, very full of feelings. And now I'd woken up to the *agape* level. At that level, I could presumably transmute the passions I had in past lives, and balance them. So I gathered all the fragments of the past lives of my twin soul and me together—here, there, in his Egyptian incarnation (I went to Karnak to settle that), as well as, most powerfully, in his Victorian incarnation. Finally, the search was truly over. But until then I wasn't free. And it was *only* then that I knew I'd have to surrender totally to the Work—the Fellowship of Isis."

The Fellowship, with its center at Clonegal Castle, was founded on the vernal equinox in 1976 by Olivia Robertson, Lawrence Durdin-Robertson, and Lawrence's late wife, Pamela Robertson. Their manifesto read:

> Growing numbers of people are rediscovering their love for the Goddess. At first, this love may seem to be no more than an inner feeling. But soon it develops; it becomes a longing to help the Goddess actively in the manifestation of Her divine plan. Thus, one hears such enquiries as, "How can I get initiated into the Mysteries of the Goddess? How can I experience a closer communion with her? Where are her nearest temples and devotees? How can I join the priesthood of the Goddess?" and many other such questions.
>
> The Fellowship of Isis has been founded to answer these needs.

Membership provides means of promoting a closer communion between the Goddess and each member, both singly and as part of a larger group.

The Fellowship is organized on a democratic basis. All members have equal privileges within it, whether as a single member or part of an Iseum or Lyceum.

The Fellowship respects the freedom of conscience of each member. There are no vows required or commitments to secrecy. All Fellowship activities are optional, and members are free to resign or rejoin at their own choice.

The Fellowship reverences all manifestations of Life. The Rites exclude any form of sacrifice, whether actual or symbolic. Nature is revered and conserved.

The Fellowship accepts religious toleration, and is not exclusivist. Members are free to maintain other religious allegiances. Membership is open to all of every religion, tradition, and race. Children are welcomed, subject to parental consent.

The Fellowship believes in the promotion of Love, Beauty, and Abundance. No encouragement is given to asceticism.

The Fellowship seeks to develop psychic gifts, happiness, and compassion for all life.

The ecumenical nature of this nonprofit organization reveals itself in a membership that includes Protestants, Catholics, Jews, Hindus, Buddhists, Shintoists, Cabalists, Spiritualists, and Wiccan and pagan worshipers of all kinds. "People join because they agree with our manifesto," says Olivia, "but of course it's up to them to interpret it." Individual members of the Fellowship of Isis, range from a coal miner in Newcastle to a police constable in Cameroon, a Jesuit priest who works in the Vatican Library to a Cherokee chief of the Etowa Clan, a poet in London to a professor in Tokyo—as well as the occasional person from Novosibirsk, Siberia, or Haifa, Israel.

For obvious reasons, some of the members of the Fellowship of Isis have asked to remain unlisted in the Fellowship's annual directory and the *Isian News*. This lively newsletter for Fellowship subscribers, at ten dollars a year, lists in its eighteen or so pages the names of new members and the more than four hundred temples of the Goddess, called Lyceums and Iseums, throughout the world. It also furnishes news and messages from members ("Yes, the Priesthood of Isis is indeed reborn in Sweden. *Evoe Isis myria Nomis!* We had a fantastic rite by Attunement in our home here in Stockholm"); gives accounts of members' psychic experiences ("Several days following my Ordination as Priestess of Freya, I was suddenly aware of a new Presence in my life, and discovered this to be a Valkyrie named Breka. She gives me training in a whole way of living"); pays respect to the community of the Animal Family of Isis ("Christi, 11-year-old dog, death/transformation—R. N., USA"; "Puca Nathair, a pure white pony who has a great spirit, friend of S. O'D. of Ireland"; "Wilfred & Jorat, cream-coloured rats, in Spirit world—M. H., England"); and presents in every issue a text of a mystery, an initiation, a rite, or, most often, an oracle of a Goddess who has been invoked by Olivia ("Divine Isis, Goddess of Ten Thousand Names, I invoke Your Grace. . . . Come to our temple, O Goddess: dwell in our shrine: make our hearth Your altar: our hearts Your home").

With the founding of the Fellowship of Isis, Olivia and Lawrence, priestess and priest of Isis, claimed that the priesthood of the Fellowship was hereditary in source, through the Robertson of Strachloch line, back to the Goddess Isis herself! "Any Celt or Gael could claim descent from Isis," Olivia gladly explains. "The priestly line comes to us from the Egyptian Princess Scota, 'the dark one,' the daughter of the Pharaoh Cincris. And Scota was hereditary Daughter of Isis through her descent from Isis and Osiris. She was given in marriage to a Scythian named Nel, well versed in wizardry. They left Egypt, founded colleges of learning, and she bore a son named Gaelglas—I picture him having red hair, I'm *sure* he had red hair. Gaelglas later declared that all of his children should be called Gaels, and Scota herself gave her name to Greater Scotia [Ireland] and to Lesser Scotia [Scotland].

"The only reason *we* can do it nicely is that my grandfather had ourselves matriculated by Lord Lyon in 1907—it cost two thousand pounds at that time to do so—right back to King Duncan of Scotland. But of course other people are just as well connected to that line of Gaels; they just don't happen to have it all writ down. Our certification got up as far as my grandfather, Herbert Robertson, M.P., in 1907. But because my brother Derry was granted the barony of Strachloch from the Irish chief herald, it's therefore been brought right back down to Derry. Though when *he* passes on, his son, David, who lives in a wing of the castle with his family, will have to get himself redone again. That would be easy, since it's just one person or two to go back to. But going back to Scota is expensive!

"You know, our family has been here since 1625, on and off; and before that, way before King Duncan, we were Irish. We belonged to the Clan Donnachaidh [Duncan] until we moved to Scotland in 1314. We are so ancient Irish that the people in this country can't really object. An orthodox Protestant man was recently complaining to me about our goings-on, and I told him that we didn't have any major problems with the Catholics. 'Of *course* not,' he said, 'it's not *them* that you've left!'

"And I suppose he's right. The most conducive place for us to be is in a Catholic country, because they still have the old mysteries—the mystery of the Mass, which is the mystery of Dionysus, and then they still practice the seven sacraments, the holy anointing of oil, and they have Maria—we're halfway there to *them!* I myself am always quoting Jesus—'The letter killeth, but the spirit giveth life'—not because I'm sucking up to Jesus or sounding goody-goody, but because I believe them and find them so *handy.* I know the feminine aspect is denigrated in Catholicism. But according to it, all attributes of the Feminine are embodied in God the Holy Ghost. And if they don't call her She, they should!"

It has occasionally been rumored by the tabloids and by uninformed pietistic souls that Clonegal Castle is a magnet for necromancy, witchcraft, and ghosts. A local priest once denounced the village of Clonegal, with a baleful nod in the direction of the castle, as "a Babylon." To which Olivia responded, "Bad vibrations belong to the sexually promiscuous, but there can also be bad vibes with a good churchgoer—and all because some *white* witches have visited us. We totally disapprove of promiscuity. We don't have orgies, we have *ecstasies!*"

Although the woman who resides in the castle gatehouse has placed a large leaf over the private parts of a Greek statue near her dwelling—in order to protect her family, she says—the village of Clonegal itself has grown used to the enchanted castle in its midst.

"Ah, Clonegal," exclaims Olivia, "such a dear, furry old place! We have, I hope, a sense of humor, and we get on very well with the local residents. We're a part of the Clonegal Development Society; the football club uses our field. We love Clonegal, and we're interested in the healing properties here."

Running alongside the gently flowing River Derry, Clonegal consists of a street of small houses, a bed-and-breakfast, a pub, a couple of grocery stores, a tiny post office, and one red public phone on the side of the road. The village is close both to Bunclody, the nearest large town, and the prediluvian Mount Leinster, with its smooth granite bluffs. There are countless sheep, looking from afar like tiny white boulders grazing amid heather and furze;

dairy cattle everywhere; and endless fields of corn, potatoes, tur-
nips, wheat, and barley. Olivia thinks of this whole bountiful valley as a "fairy-zone" whose power extends seven miles in a circle,
with Clonegal Castle at its center.

"As a child I regarded it as heaven," she says. She recalls fre-
quent meetings with a remarkable man. "We had a real Merlin,"
she declares, "a Mr. Daniel Fox. He was an Irishman who had
been in the British army. But when I knew him, he was a hermit
who lived in the woods in an ancient secret holy place where there
was an altar, a well, a stone, a bee's rock, and a fairy's seat. He
said that he was psychic, and he suddenly *knew* that he was when
he witnessed a man who was being buried start to walk around.
He saw the spirit people everywhere; he would see and hear them,
he said, as they rose at early dawn. My brothers Derry and Esmond would go off shooting rabbits. But I'd stay and inquire,
'Would you tell me about *them*, Mr. Fox?' And I was flattered
when he did. He saw the ancient Irish, the Tuatha De Danann,
and he got me through to the Tir Nan Og, the land of the forever
young. The parish curate was worried that my parents' dear children would be influenced by that man, so he warned them. But
they very wisely allowed us to go on a donkey cart from time to
time to visit this ancient sage, certain that we would out-grow all
of that."

In spite of her upbringing, she didn't. And when she was
older, she remembered hearing stories about a meteorite that had
fallen sometime at the end of the nineteenth century behind the
castle grounds and had glowed for two years—an auspicious sign,
Olivia and Lawrence would later believe, for the founding of a
spiritual center in their family castle, a place that would be devoted to the protection of the earth, care for children, love of
animals, the awakening of true seeing and true hearing in human
beings, and the worship of the Goddess in all her manifestations.

. . .

"You worship all the goddesses," I mention to Olivia one afternoon over lunch. "So why the Fellowship of Isis? Why *Isis*?"

We are seated in the castle's dining room, which contains the original granite fireplace from 1625, through which a hatch has been built so that dishes can be passed on trolleys into and out of the old-fashioned kitchen. To the right of the fireplace is a stained glass window made in 1870 that commemorates in heraldry a number of ancestors, including Richard and Frances Durdin, who ran away from Ireland in the eighteenth century because of their illegal mixed marriage (he was a Protestant, she a Catholic) and founded the city of Huntington, Pennsylvania. To the left of the fireplace is the family silver collection with its trophies. On the walls are Bedouin tent-hangings from Tunisia. An aspidistra is sitting in the center of the dining table.

"The reason I take Isis," says Olivia, who today is wearing a crimson velvet bolero, "is that she's a universal goddess—the Isis of Ten Thousand Names. She includes them all: Demeter, Lakshmi, Kwan Yin, Dana, Ngame, Maria."

"On the porch at the back of the castle," I observe, "there are stone statues of four Christian saints and two angels, above which one can see the protecting, outspread wings of a clay Isis."

"I always say that I regard Christianity as a rebirth of the Isis mysteries," Olivia asserts. "To me, Maria *was* Isis, Christ *was* both Osiris and then Horus after Osiris' resurrection. The decline and subsequent strengthening of the sun, source of all life on earth, is enacted in the birth of the infant Horus—the Hawk Sun God of the East—as well as of the baby Jesus. The winter solstice is the festival for both nativities. Also, both Isis and Maria gave birth not through man but through God.

"You know, the most remarkable relationship of Isis and Maria occurred during the physical sky phenomena that took place near Cairo from April 1968 on through 1970. Heralded by lights in the sky, the form of a woman with halo, made of dazzling light, appeared regularly over the Coptic church of St. Mary at On [now named Zeitun], which was where Maria was believed to have rested with the infant Jesus during their flight into Egypt. There are photographs of the apparitions seen by thousands of Muslims and others. The important fact is that the Muslims took the woman, sometimes holding a baby, to be Fatima with her son, Ali. The Christians took her to be the Virgin Mary holding the infant Jesus. But there were many there who recognized Isis with Horus. Which was she? All of them, I believe. Don't you think so too, Derry?"

Olivia's brother is seated opposite her, wearing a buttoned-up black overcoat to protect himself from the castle drafts as he slowly eats his vegetarian Irish stew and a salad and responds with what sounds like an indistinct yes.

"I should tell you that Derry thinks that the Goddess Isis is preeminent, while I accept the complementary nature of Isis and Osiris. Isn't that true, Derry?"

Derry eventually nods.

"It's that rheumatism and laryngitis of his," she again explains to me, "as well as his depression about his late wife. Don't worry, Derry," she remarks encouragingly and lovingly to her brother, "you're on the road to recovery!"

"You know," says Olivia, turning back to me, "one can transmute passion through a *greater* passion . . . so that through the intense feeling of grief or sorrow, you can go deeply through the dark tunnel of those emotions—that's the Osirian mystery, really—and come out to a greater love. You've lost your wife"— she glances at Derry—"and now you've found the Goddess who includes your wife and *all* women. She's far *greater* than your wife—your wife falls away like a leaf. And by finding the greater, you find the heart of God. Now, let's say a woman's husband is dead, and she's totally grief-stricken. Funnily enough, the more grief-stricken she is, the more she's redeemed. Because through that heartbreak, she finds her husband in Dionysus, in Christ, in Osiris. . . . So the man falls in love with the Goddess, the woman sees the God in the man."

"What do you think of Isis and Osiris as a love story?" I ask.

"I think that the story of Isis and Osiris is *the* love story. You look through Greek mythology, and there doesn't seem to be a happy marriage. Jupiter and Juno are fighting all the time. Oddly enough, Mars was respectably married, but he committed adultery with Venus. They're more like modern Americans." She laughs. "I'm sorry to be nasty, but of course today two out of three marriages in England break up, so everyone is copying you! Or take Rama and Sita. Sita was abducted by Ravana the demon, and her husband was pretty horrible, I think. He made her go through an ordeal by fire, because although he believed in her chastity, the people didn't. But it rather puts me off Rama.

"With Isis and Osiris, however, we have a harmonious polarity: brother and sister, twin souls, husband and wife. They could be all relationships. If I'm dealing with very spiritual people who understand the idea of twin souls, I'll refer to Isis and Osiris as sister and brother. But in a more mundane situation I talk about them as wife and husband.

"Now, Osiris is imprisoned in a coffin by his brother Set, the skillful artist, who has painted jolly scenes of glamour girls and hunting on it. But it's obvious that what Osiris is trapped in is *his own body*. Osiris is lured into incarnation by a sort of focusing of interest. And by focusing interest on a particular aspect of persona—I'm Miss Smith, I'm Mr. Smith—you lose everything else.

"Later, Osiris is imprisoned in a tree—he's a part of all nature and can't get out. He *is* a body and he *is* a tree—we *all* are. After he's freed from that, he's dismembered. We *all* are, you see. We're so dismembered, we're all in bits. Which leads to fragmentation. It's like losing yourself in a succession of soap operas, identifying with one character or another and forgetting yourself. The parts of Osiris were scattered all over Egypt—his heart in Abydos, a leg in Philae, the backbone in Luxor. So when we ourselves focus on just one particular bit of consciousness, we too lose all the rest.

"The aim, therefore, in what I might call the Isian consciousness is to place yourself in the hub of the wheel where you are one with Osiris and Isis. You're not some kind of hermaphrodite—you're the mode of *man* or the mode of *woman*, you don't deny your own many incarnations, you just make them all a part of yourself. Just as Osiris is made whole. He's been drawn into incarnation, being this person and that—he sinks into death, he's rescued by divine union with the Goddess, he ascends into the sky as a God, and someone else, his son Horus, then takes his place.

"And the Goddess goes through the same thing. When Isis loses Osiris, she proceeds to put him together in order to put *herself* together. Don't you think so? Retrieving their past memories, past arguments, past lives. The idea, you see, is to bring about union—to get to Deity in your own way, through your own true conscience, to the core of yourself.

"Our ceremonies here at the castle try to bring people to a state of wholeness. We try to do that by enabling them to act as channels for the Deific Presence. You see, the main difference between great drama and the ancient mysteries was that the mysteries were not for an audience, but rather brought each performer into meaningful participation with the enacted drama. The neophyte identified with Psyche in her quest for Eros, with Orpheus seeking Eurydice, with Isis searching for Osiris. According to his or her own development, the neophyte underwent each deepening layer of consciousness—stage one, two, three. Each stage brought its peculiar ordeal. And according to the neophyte's capacity, he or she succeeded or failed.

"Now, I used to think that a person could only achieve a mystical experience by embodying the principal characters of, say, Isis or Osiris. Then I discovered that you could attain as much by being the jackal god, Anubis. Anyone can have a mystical experience by being *any* of the characters of a mystery play, because *all* of them are divine. We understand the passions of Set, the tenderness of Nephthys—all these are within ourselves. We're all in the same boat. All of us are suffering somewhere; and if we aren't, then *that* is the greatest sorrow, because we haven't yet learned to.

"In our Temple of Isis, my aim is to create rituals that teach the laws of expanding consciousness. These dramas aren't ritual magic in the practical sense, and they aren't intended to produce effects on the physical environment. Rather, they're meant to affect the minds and feelings of those taking part in group participation. For what is life as we know it but a group dreaming? And the drama of Isis and Osiris is about awakening into who we really are."

The rites, ordinations, and mysteries of the Fellowship of Isis are performed in the Temple of Isis, which occupies the entire basement area of Clonegal Castle. It is approached through a double door in the hall at the rear of the castle, in front of which stand two temple guardians with swords, originally from a Buddhist temple in Burma, and above which is a powerful mask of Neith, the Egyptian goddess of war and hunting, carved in boxwood by Derry's son, David, a sculptor in his late thirties.

After opening the door, you make your way down a flight of granite steps and find yourself in an astonishing, teeming, dizzying

world. To the left as you enter is a large Tibetan gong, an amal-
gam of eleven metals that when struck produces a seemingly endless series of evanescent frequencies. Through a heavy iron gate
you come to a seventeen-foot well that draws from a spring once
sacred to the Druids. Olivia considers the water to have healing
properties and has dedicated the well to Brighid, the Irish goddess
of poetry, healing, and springs, and she always suggests that visitors put some drops of the icy water on their foreheads in order
to experience "a tingling effect that seems to awaken the third
eye."

In the dim basement light you move slowly on stone floors
covered with rugs through what were once the castle's pantries,
sculleries, wine cellars, and the former dungeon, now transformed
into the Chapel of the Mothers. Its barrel-vaulted roof serves to
represent the womb, and it contains drawings and masks of the
Great Mother as well as scores of children's toys and small objects
of the animal, vegetable, and mineral realms.

Walking on, you almost trip over two enormous multicolored
stuffed canvas dragons, affectionately called Yin and Yang, twisted
lengthwise around four of the temple's nine columns. "They are
our pews!" Olivia says of these fantastic, sinuous creatures, made
for and given to the Fellowship by the sister of Brigitte Bardot—
one of the goddesses of *our* century.

Wandering through the temple, you come across five chapels
and twelve shrines of the zodiac which honor goddesses from all
over the world. By the light of several stained glass windows and
flickering candles in many tiny alcoves, you can see a gallimaufry
of literally thousands of objects—some kitsch, some works of art
of ancient and modern sources—including shells, feathers, am-
phorae, crystals, necklaces, chalices, trays, icons, clay pottery, wall
hangings, gold cloth, visionary paintings, china birds, and masks,
some found, some bought, some made by the Durdin-Robertsons

and by Fellowship of Isis members from Finland to Australia, from Nigeria to Japan.

Finally, at the High Altar, the Holy of Holies, you behold in a special crowned niche a carved statuette of the Isis of Ten Thousand Names holding the sun disk between the horns of the moon. "She started as the Madonna of the Aquarian Age," Olivia explains, "but now she's Isis. She was also naked at first. My nephew David carved her out of a yew tree when he was fifteen, and I said, 'David'—I was rather proper in those days—'Molly won't clean the chapel if you have a naked Mary.' David was very annoyed. So I said, 'Why don't you dress her in water?' So he added her robes of water."

Candles surround the goddess, and on either side of her are two black figures, one representing Queen Tehani of Mu (the lost continent) and the other the Goddess Ngame of Nigeria, where more than a third of the Fellowship of Isis' members reside. The former goddess is covering her breasts, the latter exposing them—"a sign of queenship," Olivia explains, adding, "You know, my second cousin Robert Graves, through a series of psychic happenings, was inspired by the Goddess Ngame to write *The White Goddess*. And in doing so, he himself inspired the creation of a great Temple of Ngame in Nigeria, run by the famous healer and writer on the occult, the Right Reverend Archpriest Michael Okoruwa, of our Fellowship of Isis priesthood. About eight hundred people attend Michael's healing rituals every Sunday in his temple courtyard, with its two large statues of Isis and Ngame. Oh, that Lady knew what She was doing, getting through to Graves!"

There are liturgical items on the altar: a sistrum, incense, holy water from Brighid's Well, holy oil for consecration and ordination, a crystal, a scarab from the Nile. "We have eight candles rising into a pyramid shape," Olivia remarks. "Eight is our number: eight-pointed star, eight-pointed year [referring to the eight festivals of the Celtic year]. On the windowsills are bottles with colored fluids that let through healing rays, as well as a large caldron containing different herbs for aromatherapy. And our ever-living flame is a red lamp of Brighid—a flickering candle that's meant to be lit all the time . . . though sometimes it isn't."

It is a late afternoon at the candlelit High Altar, and Olivia Robertson and Lawrence Durdin-Robertson, attired in priestly garb, have gathered together a group of visiting Fellowship of Isis members to complete the enactment and tape recording of the Mystery of the Awakening of Osiris, begun upstairs a half-hour ago in the castle's drawing room. In addition to Olivia, who performs the roles of the Priestess and Narrator, and Derry, as Priest, the participating devotees, carrying copies of the text of the mystery, include Debe Nix, the founder of the Isis of Phylae Lyceum in Destin, Florida, as Isis; John Merron, an earth mysteries researcher from London, as Osiris, Horus, and Harpocrates; Caroline Wise and Steve Wilson, cofounders of the Lyceum of the Isis of Time and Space in London, as Hathor and as the Priest, Thoth, Set, and Anubis respectively; Joan, Countesse de Frenay, a long-time family friend of the Durdin-Robertsons who is a Tarot card reader from Dublin, as Nephthys and Maat; and me, as Witness. The votaries are garbed in robes, stoles, and identifying regalia: jackal's head, hawk's head, cow's horns. I have been allowed to attend with the request that I wear a white robe to the ceremony. Thus adorned, I stand against a temple wall near a small gas heater and watch and listen while Olivia as the Priestess offers incense to Isis. (Osiris, played by John Merron, has meanwhile enshrouded himself in a black veil and lain down in the nearby Chapel of the Mothers.

PRIESTESS: We offer incense to the Goddess Isis and to the God Osiris. May we be blessed as we enact their mystery.

PRIEST: Lament with us. The God Osiris is dead. (*Priest puts out the candle's light.*) He lieth in a chest made from the erica tree by his brother, the God Set, the skillful crafts-man. Set painted it with colored pictures marvelous to be-hold, and the heart of Osiris yearned for it and he lay in it. But the chest was measured to the form of the body of Osiris so that he could not escape. And so he died. Yet what dreams hath he in this sleep of death?

PRIESTESS: He liveth in dreams: he fleeth, yet his enemy killeth him many times. He is dismembered, and each fragment is scattered concealed throughout the Two Lands of Khem. And as he sleepeth, his wife protecteth him.

[*Olivia changes to her role as* NARRATOR]: Suddenly, from the shadows of the temple, a woman most beautiful in soul, but full of grief, her head sprinkled with ashes, steps forth. *This is Isis.*

(*Debe Nix approaches the company, robed and crowned as Isis.*)

ISIS: I repel his enemies and cause the deeds of the mis-chief-maker to retreat in the power of my mouth. I take action for my husband: while he is lost in dreams, I seek him without turning. I rove through the lands as the wail-ing kite without rest until I find him and awaken him to life. I provide shade for his lost soul with my feathers, and I create wind with my wings that I may bring my husband to peace. I strengthen the weakness of him who is tired of heart. I have borne an heir, Horus, and suckled the infant in solitude—the place where he is unknown.

NARRATOR: Now Isis conducts the great search for Osiris. She wanders through this cavernous temple, She looks into many nooks and crannies and places . . . but in vain. Her husband is dead. She looks from place to place, and as She does so, all the company mourns the death of Osiris, and utters the immemorial cry "Osiris is dead. May Isis bring him to life!" They chant the word *Isis!*

ALL CHANT: Isis!

NARRATOR: And as they chant, all those who are bereaved, who have lost those they love in the darkness of death, take up the chant, and then they chant *Osiris* to make himself known, to be restored.

ALL CHANT: Osiris! Osiris!

NARRATOR: The company now follows Isis, who sinks upon the ground in desperation. Let us now all meditate, and seek to see the form and vision of our own lost loves.

Silent meditation [with the heartbreaking, muffled sound of Derry sobbing]

NARRATOR: Lo, as all those who suffer grief or loss have strengthened Isis in her search, now, in her wandering, she comes upon a dark and gloomy dungeon—the Chapel of the Mothers—with a light in the sky, so that a beam of light falls upon the body of Osiris. And it is imprisoned in a tree!

PRIEST: Osiris in his sleep of death heareth the words of Isis and of her search. Memory cometh unto him.

OSIRIS (*speaking haltingly, grievingly*): Lo! Love awakeneth in my heart for my wife. I know myself to be Osiris. Yet am I but the living dead when I have knowledge, but cannot move even one finger. Who will call me into life with magic words of power?

NARRATOR: Now comes the mystical dance of Isis, which calls forth the inner power of the God Ra, as a serpent bite coursing through her blood; which calls forth Buto, the cobra, within her own body, and therefore within the body of Osiris. She dances, joined by all the company. *Dance* with movements you once knew, and draw up from the depths of the earth, where Osiris is imprisoned, the inner fire of the earth. Feel it rising up your body, up your spine, drying your tears, up to your heart. *Feel this!* (*Rattles sistrum. Company does slow, sinuous dance.*)

And as she does so, suddenly Isis remembers she is not a weeping, mourning widow, but a goddess! And as she does that, she lifts up her arms to the sky, and white power comes down upon her head. It descends through her in an inverted cone and reaches her heart, and then her heart awakens, and the eight-pointed star of Isis shines about her. Now that she herself *knows* she is a goddess within, she is empowered to awaken the dead. She calls to Osiris and to all humanity to awaken to their own innate divinity.

ISIS: Come to thy house, come to thy house, O God, come to thy house, that thou mayest see me. I am thy wife, whom thou lovest; thou shalt not part from me, O fair youth; come to thy house. Yet doth my heart yearn after thee and mine eyes desire thee. . . . Come to thy house and to thy wife. I am twin of thy soul, for we two are children of the Goddess Nut, whose starry body archeth across the sky of night. Thou art in verity the shepherd with the crook that guardeth the starry flocks of darkness. With my white star I follow thee as thou sinkest into the depths of the Western Ocean at the end of the world. Gods and men have buried their faces toward thee and weep for thee together. I call after them and weep. Yet am I thy wife, whom thou didst love. My lover! My lover!

NARRATOR: As she speaks, Osiris begins to awaken from that death which we call existence on earth.

OSIRIS: I see myself in many dreams with many names and many forms; I hear the call of my beloved Isis; and I call my many selves unto me and I name them. For all are Osiris. May all of these be awakened with me, for are they not my kin?

NARRATOR: As Osiris slowly awakens from the dreams that we all live, into memory of past incarnations, Isis *also* begins to remember, and falls on her knees as memory comes—memories of many lives and memories of heaven. Let us join her in this awakening of past and future. (*Turns on second tape machine, and once again we hear the ambient strains of flute, harp, and synthesizer music.*)

Awaken, awaken the souls of the dead! We begin to

see the form of those we love, coming to us from Amenti, no longer invisible. The dead awaken. They live. And we who *think* we live are awakening into life. We are priestesses in Egypt, priests in Greece, lovers in Babylon, students in Atlantis, monks, nuns, sinners, saints: the great awakening is at hand! Sorrow is turned into wonder, as arms are stretched to us. To aid us awaken, we need their love. The mightier form of the goddesses now are gleaming in the distance, like far-off mountains. And they are surrounded by aureoles of color, of beauty. We begin to see the stars. And we [*in a whisper*] *awaken.* The awakening is so strange, we are afraid we are going to forget what we were five minutes ago. We can see, we can hear, we can laugh. For this moment of time is all I experience. We learn the justice of Maat, we understand the passions of Set, the gentleness of Nephthys, the love of Isis. For all of these are within ourselves. *Feel that!*

(Meditation. Quiet sounds of music.)

NARRATOR: Friends! We become aware after our meditation that we are still in the Temple of Isis, gazing upon the dead body of Osiris, who is slowly awakening, remembering many lives, many loves, wrongdoings, well-doings, violence, and gentleness. But now as we begin to awaken, we can see the forms of those great beings we call goddesses and gods, those who have experienced all that we have, have suffered all that we have, and have ascended into glory, into immortal life. We see the Goddess Maat, she who is the judge, she who is the epitome of justice, and she is a priestess in pure white, with long black hair, and she's holding forth the feather of truth. Note, this feather is *not* rigid, for it responds to every breeze of new realization. Maat speaks.

MAAT: A swallow brought news of the death of Osiris to Isis, and so she set forth to save him. May swallows and all winged creatures live forever. So sayeth the Goddess Maat.

(Seven other gods and goddesses—Set, Harpocrates, Anubis, Horus, Nephthys, Hathor, and Thoth—now step forth to bless scorpions and vultures, fishermen and children for having aided Isis in her search for Osiris.)

NARRATOR: Now cometh the dance of resurrection! Isis leads it. She is seeking the many parts of the fragmented Osiris from many lives. And she dances to the east, to the south, to the west, and to the north. And as she dances, she calls forth the soul of Osiris long lost in Egypt, lost in China, lost in India, lost in Greece, lost in Rome, lost in ancient France, lost in Eire, lost in Albion. And as she dances, the soul of Osiris draws its many parts into one mighty whole. And we who have etheric vision gaze upon the coffin of Osiris, and we begin to see his many forms appear: the priest in Babylon, the Pharaoh in Egypt, the artist in Europe, the warrior in Ethiopia, the holy man in Tibet. And all these figures begin to merge into one. . . . Now you see Osiris with rainbow colors, you see the company with their beautiful auras, but you do not know that they see *your* beauty. For we can only see the beauty of deity in others, not in ourselves. Save through the mirror of Hathor. So we honor and respect all beings, for we now see their glory. *Feel this.*

All now stand in a circle around the sleeping Osiris [*whispering and motioning to the devotees to circle Osiris*], and they hold their hands with palms facing outward to empower Isis for what she is about to do. She is not going to resurrect a man, she is going to resurrect a god! The priest declareth—

PRIEST: Wise are the deities! The search is ended. Isis hath found Osiris within the tree.

PRIESTESS: Isis opened the painted chest, and laying her face on the face of her husband, and her heart upon his heart, she kissed him, and she wet his face with her tears. The winged Isis caused breath to enter into the body. And she breathed into his nostrils and his mouth the breath of life. And behold, he lived again!

NARRATOR *(declaiming)*: And all the company cries out, "Hail, Isis; Osiris is risen from the dead!"

DEITIES: Hail, Isis; Osiris is risen from the dead!

NARRATOR *(quietly and gently)*: Isis now lies on his body, brow to brow, heart to heart, palm to palm, leg to leg. And the life of Isis entereth fully into the body of Osiris, awakened as a man, and now awakening as a god. . . . Feel within yourself the breath of Isis, her brow upon your brow, her heart upon your heart, her body upon yours, her palms upon the palms of your hands, for Isis is your mother, for Isis is all mothers. She hath given you life, and she giveth you now new life within, rebirth into knowledge of your own divinity. *Awaken!*

(While Olivia has been speaking, Isis has taken a vessel of water, removed Osiris' veil and sprinkled his brow with water, placed her hand on his heart, then bent down and kissed him on the brow.)

ISIS: Osiris, awake!

(Priest lights the candle. Osiris rises, faces Isis, and they raise the palms of their hands toward each other.)

DEITIES: Isis and Osiris united!

NARRATOR: And as we chant, the chant is taken up by beings from the invisible world, as the spirits of woman and of man, of animals, of birds, of reptiles, of fishes, and of trees awaken into their own eternal life.

(Priestess rattles sistrum.)

PRIEST: The miracle is accomplished and all things are renewed. Osiris is risen from the dead! Glory and praise and thanksgiving be unto Isis, for hers is the palm of victory!

OSIRIS: Who are these glorious beings that standeth about me? I behold my wife, Isis, and her sister Nephthys. My brother Set holdeth forth to me a garment of twelve colors. Horus with the Eye of Morning greeteth me, and Hathor of the cow's head gives me the love of the mother. Before me is Maat with the feather of truth. On my right hand is Anubis with the scales of justice, and on my left is Thoth of the hidden wisdom. My brother Harpocrates of the mysteries holds one finger to his mouth, enjoining silence.

NARRATOR: All now surround Osiris and plant upon his brow a kiss of recognition, for he is now of the company of gods because he knows he *is* a god, and Isis remembers she is a *goddess*, and her sister Hathor places upon her head the diadem of Isis.

PRIESTESS: Let us meditate upon the key of Isis that opens the doors of the upper world of the winged ones, and the doors of Amenti, the underworld, where Osiris reigns with crook and winnowing flail.

NARRATOR: And the priestess holds aloft the key of life, the ankh, key to all spheres. We are aware of a sudden change, we can see the key of life, a loop over a cross, shining brilliantly. But we begin to see the company become faded as if caught in the wisps of incense. We see the gods and goddesses, and now they no longer look like gods and goddesses. The deities are withdrawing from those through whom they came. And we watch the priesthood now divested of hawk's head and cow's horns, their insignia, seated to partake of the holy feast of the mysteries. And we watch and see that they are being given bread and wine.

PRIEST (*giving each participant a piece of bread*): From Osiris take immortal wheat, that your soul may awaken and gain the harvest of many lives.

PRIESTESS (*placing water on the brow of each participant*): From Isis receive the water of life. May you know your immortality. (*Faces participants, arms raised in Isis position.*) May all beings awaken into eternal reality. May you go forth in peace.

NARRATOR (*speaking in hushed tones into the microphone as she turns away from the participants*): But now she is only a voice, for we are withdrawing from this holy ceremony, and we only hear the words of the priesthood, giving thanks to the deities. We are rising now with the incense through this misty castle, now into the darkness of Samhain—of Halloween Eve. We now see all the stars around us as we rise into the sky, above the castle, above the trees. And we too feel we have received the bread of life, the wine of life.

But there is something rather odd. *You* are in another time and place, aren't you? Come back now to your own time and place with *me* . . . and remember to drink a glass of water afterwards . . . and make sure you don't go into traffic for about a half-hour—you may feel a little dreamy. . . . Write us anytime: Fellowship of Isis, Clonegal Castle, Enniscorthy, Eire.

"I know your parents tried at all costs to keep you from becoming an actress," I remark to Olivia the following afternoon. "But when you were a child, did you ever make up and act in your own plays?"

"I *loved* acting and getting up charades as a child, yes," Olivia says. "My brothers and sister and I acted little plays—little ghost stories and such. I wrote and directed them. Why do you ask?"

"Because no matter how silly or ludicrous a work like the Mystery of the Awakening of Osiris might seem to certain sarcastic and sneering types," I observe, "there's no gainsaying its charm, naiveté, and childlike openheartedness . . . and the truly moving way it tells and presents the myth."

"My texts are taken from ancient sources," Olivia states, "the Pyramid Texts, the *Egyptian Book of the Dead,* and Plutarch in the Osiris mystery, for example. We have a marvelous library here at the castle, you know. In a way our ceremonies *are* an education, because I think people should know the stories of Plato's cave and Virgil's Golden Age. And I'm trying to put all cultures and faiths into a mosaic, which I hope won't turn out to be a bad cocktail since they connect to something we all share, like the sun, the moon, the stars.

"But we do make up the gestures—I mean, we know nothing about how they did them at Eleusis—so I hope we're getting it right! And I do add my own things, like the extended narration and the meditations you heard me improvise yesterday for the Osiris mystery. I'm . . . sort of *inspired.* I have to be honest and say that it's channeled *through* me. I do things inspirationally, but I never lose consciousness. I get heightened, not lessened; I don't get dim, I get more!

"Certainly people sometimes try to take the mickey out of what we do. St. Paul said he was a fool for Christ's sake, and doubtless he was accused of being dotty. Those who think us fools are themselves foolish—wise in their own folly. Because they are neglecting what is real and chasing after the transient. As I said before, we *have* grown up, but we've kept our childhood with us. So of course there's a sense of the childlike in our ceremonies; the element of the ludicrous must *always* be apparent in the element of the sacred. When Spike Milligan was cremated, his friends from *The Goon Show* came out of the crematorium playing religious music, and all of a sudden, just as they got outside, they began playing and singing, 'I want to be happy/But I won't be happy/Till I make you happy, too!' Do you see what I mean?

"I used to tell fortunes—always do—by the palm of the hand. And I was always surrounded by a sea of faces, of hands held out to me, imploring, 'Help us!' Why? Because I somehow was able to make them feel wonderful. Because I don't *laugh* if there are ten Nefertitis in a room. *Every* woman is a Nefertiti, in the sense that Nefertiti herself identified with Isis. And I found that I could see the Goddess in these women, and the God in the man."

Her energy unflagging as always, Olivia is again having tea with me in the conservatory. And again she is clothed in red—a scarlet shawl wrapped over a black polo-neck sweater. "Flaming red I wear for vitality," she informs me. "I've got to be vital and active this week, but when you're gone, I'll lapse into peacock blue—something gentle and quiet."

"What is your daily routine like?" I ask.

"I get up at half-past five," she says, "take a *hot* bath, then go to the temple, meditate for an hour, lying flat on my back and listening to classical music and going on a trip. And I *don't* mean drugs! This keeps me happy. And then I get my instructions."

"What kind of instructions?"

"Well . . ." Olivia pauses. "Let's say that the previous night in the temple I've invoked a goddess whose oracle I feel guided to receive; I'll strengthen that communion in my sleep state. And when I've returned to the temple the next morning and sit by Brighid's Well, I receive a flow of power, which feels like an on-rush of silver-white light through my head, or a golden glow in my spine and heart, according to the attributes of the goddess invoked. Truth is related for me with white power, love with gold. Three hours later, after a period of meditation, I perform a simple rite in the drawing room. I light a candle and burn incense. I put well water on my forehead and ask to receive the oracle. Then, with my mind as blank as I can make it, I sit at my desk and wait for inspiration. When the oracle comes, it comes swiftly, without stop, and I write as I receive it."

"You mentioned drugs before," I say. "What is your attitude toward them?"

"Drugs burn out the chakras," Olivia responds. "For a time it can be like turning on a light bulb—an electrician can do it from the outside. But it's not coming from the source; therefore it can't glow. Our brain can make all the lysergic acid we want—I regard it as the forbidden fruit of the Bible. You're told not to eat the fruit of life, but that doesn't mean you won't *ever* eat it, rather that Adam and Eve weren't ready for it. You don't go up and pluck the fruit; you lean your back against the bough, and it should be *in* you and come up your spine—natural growth. And *then* you're in touch with all lives, all beings; *then* you're developing the way the deities intended you to.

"Here at Clonegal Castle we use grapes, not wine, in our rituals, though we do use wine afterward at our parties. *These* grapes." She points to the vine overhead. "Occasionally, I will have a pint at the village pub. And I have to confess that at one party here I did accept a bit of Bailey's Irish Cream—I thought it was too priggish not to!"

"Some people," I say, "imagine that you practice some kind of sex initiations here at Clonegal Castle."

"The answer," replies Olivia, "is *no*. One man came looking for that, and he complained, 'Well, what's Isis about if it's not sex?' And he never came back. People think that if a religion *doesn't* say, 'Thou shalt not . . .' But of course there *are* various layers to the Fellowship. The witchcraft layer is working on that level, the fertility level, and there's nothing wrong with that. The person looking for orgies, however, has come to the wrong place. Divine ecstasy *includes* sex, but it may also mean that you're celibate. In other words, it awakens the divine fire, the divine chakras.

"I'll give you an example. I met this witch, a woman, who was terribly upset because she could no longer practice as a witch since she had had a hysterectomy. She told me, 'I can do no more.' And it wasn't having a very pleasant effect on her character. 'I've no womb, I've an empty womb,' she kept repeating. I replied, 'I can't understand what you mean. Your spiritual womb is still there, your etheric double has this beautiful hidden chakra. You have all these sacred centers within your spirit body. What does your body matter?' And she said, 'I'd never initiate anyone with a deformed body.' But I laugh at groups that won't initiate a hunchback, for example. Though *we* will. Because a hunchback is straight in the spirit world, if his *soul* is straight. We see in terms of spirit. Therefore, sex is irrelevant—immaterial and irrelevant! Hence the beautiful robes we wear in our ceremonies are the color of our auras. And we say that *that* world is the real one!"

"Although you and your ceremonies tend toward the theatrical," I say to Olivia, "I notice that you seem to treasure the simplest of devotions, too. You once wrote, 'Though we respect great temples, a simple room and grove of trees form a Matrix that protects our altar fire.'"

"The rites in a manual of mine like *Dea*," Olivia tells me, "start very simply for that devotee who, all alone, may be starting on the path to the mysteries. Those who are drawn to this path are often quite lonely. In past ages those churchmen and kings who persecuted people with psychic gifts at least acknowledged those faculties to be *real*. It's possibly more complimentary, if disagreeable, to be burned or drowned or hanged than to be incarcerated in a mental home as a patient suffering from delusions! No one likes to be thought either absurd or mad.

"Now, the creation of a shrine helps a lonely devotee to make a stronghold for the soul, where psychic development can take place without disturbance from unsympathetic family or neighbors. All that is *essential* is the power to make images with the eyes shut, or imagine beautiful words and music through the creative imagination. Of course, actual representations certainly help. In the 'Dedication of a Shrine to the Goddess Isis,' a text you'll find in my book *Dea*, the oracle proclaims, 'Wherever a devotee places my picture, my statue, two candles, incense, and a cup of water, there shall I dwell. There shall Joy, Health, and Abundance be the gifts of my eternal Love.'"

"So one can turn a room or a corner of one's room into a hall of mystery," I remark.

"Exactly!" Olivia exclaims. "But remember, what you're transforming it into isn't fantasy but *real* reality! Right now, you and I are sharing this dream. But if we could see it as a painted veil, a pale film, a play, we'd then look up and see the vine in this room as loving, and we'd see the whole story of Henry VIII at Hampton Court, and we'd see the 'true vine of life,' and we'd see the grapes surrounded by an aura. Just think of it: this is our roof, we are under our own vine, and that's eternal.

"Now look at the Italian mosaics here on the floor, with the eight-pointed stars balanced with pyramids. Look at the great urn over there with flowers in it. Look at that wicker basket and remember the people who made it by hand. Look out the windows and see the yew trees and the woods in the distance. I *know* I'm lucky to be here. But if you have only one tree to look at, then that tree could be the woods for you. Do you see?

"I once went to a particularly deadening series of occult lectures by a famous guru-teacher—teachings that were mental games that you played with yourself and that negated any enjoyment. Afterward, I remember walking along—it was summertime—and suddenly the rhythm of the universe stopped for me for a few seconds. There didn't seem any point putting one foot in front of the other any longer. I had always had a little song

and rhythm in me—always it was there. And I realized how dan-
gerous nihilistic teachings can be. I knew I needed a spiritual family, and it was only the Fellowship of Isis that had filled up that
longing for companionship. I wanted a universal family, where I
could be with my friends of *whatever* faith. I never have any use
for people who negate or denigrate other people's faiths, whether
of the Jews, the Christians, the Hindus, the Buddhists, the
witches, because they're breaking apart the religion of childhood.
Never overturn someone else's idol.

"It's said that Swami Yogananda once desired to meet a truly
holy man, but on his way he popped into a temple where they
worshiped a stone. And he sat there, quite despising those idola-
tors. Then he went off again, and was given the wrong directions.
So he decided to go back to where he'd started, and somehow he
felt guided to return to that first temple. He sat there, looking at
the stone, and suddenly it became filled with the light of God. He
realized what a mistake he'd made the first time. And from that
moment he was able to find his way quite easily. And that is how
I feel. To me, Abraham should have gone back to Ur, respected
his father's idols, those same idols he had willfully broken, dusted
them up, stuck them together with Bostik, and paid them reverence."

During my eight-day stay at Clonegal Castle, I attended several
ceremonies. In addition to the Osiris mystery, I was a witness at
an enchanting Isis wedding rite, in which Caroline Wise, covered
in a veil and wearing a dark-blue cotton robe decorated with gold
stars, and Steve Wilson, in a pale blue robe and mitre, were joined
in wedlock. Assisting in the rite were several Fellowship of Isis
members enacting the roles of a hooded Guardian of the Gate, a
robed Bard of the Druids, and two Temple Maidens in velvet

caftans. Derry was, of course, the Priest of Isis, and Olivia, wearing a golden Marian crown, took the part of Priestess-Hierophant. At the outset of the ceremony she told the bride and bridegroom, "This wedding rite is one of the most ancient in the world. It springs from the great Indian nation, from the ancient Egyptians, and from the Gaels, who all saw marriage not as an enclosure, a binding, but as a joyful union that welcomes all natures and all beings of loving heart. Even if there were other loves in the past, these are all now loved by the bride and bridegroom. You're not asked to forsake all others, you're asked to embrace all others. Therefore there's no jealousy, no envy, no hatred. For this union is a union of Isis and Osiris, of Lakshmi and Vishnu, of Eros and Psyche, of Christ and the Bride, of you and me!"

Then, on Sunday, September 23, the day before my departure, about thirty members and friends of the Fellowship of Isis came together from different parts of Ireland, England, the United States, and Australia to celebrate the autumn equinox in a Druid ritual. In the dining room, incense was burned and prayers were spoken. As Olivia exclaimed, "Strike up the beat and we will go forth!" three participants began playing an Irish air on recorder, drums, and tambourine, and the devotees—some wearing white-and-black robes, black capes, and myrtle wreaths—made their way out of the castle's front door to the nearby ruined Abbey, now known as the Temple of Dana, with its dolmen altar, flowering shrubs, and rambling roses. It is here, eight times during the year, that Olivia and Derry observe and celebrate the eight Celtic Danann seasonal holidays. And here, on a gray, windy, overcast afternoon, with leaves blowing about on this once Druidic site, an older Irish member of the Fellowship uttered a prayer in Gaelic invoking the Goddess Dana and the Tuatha De Danann and beseeching them to protect our fragile earth.

.   .   .

Later that afternoon, I got a chance to meet informally at the village pub with about fifteen of that day's participants, now dressed in their civilian clothes and blending right into the more profane setting of darts, TV, and general good cheer. Olivia too was present, sipping on a glass of her favorite Bailey's. For two hours I spoke to priests and priestesses, dames and knights of Tara, Druidesses and Druids of the Clan of Dana, and a remarkable older gentleman who, I was told, was the last survivor of the pre-Druid Megalithic Order (his title: Herenach of the Diocese of the Two Kilmares and Chief of the Name).

A producer from BBC Ulster Television who had come down to the autumn equinox celebration to do some research on the Durdin-Robertsons was also in the group. In fact, the Fellowship of Isis—its rites, ordinations, and festivals—has been the subject of about a dozen programs and documentaries that have been shown on Irish, Welsh, Scottish, and English television. A half-hour enactment of the Isis wedding rite was aired on Telefís Eireann in 1976, following the Pope's Easter Day address. The next day more than a hundred curious people showed up on the front lawn of Clonegal Castle.

"You know, the Irish aren't like the English," Olivia remarked to the BBC producer. "We're born with footlights around us! But wherever we come from, most of us are stagestruck and like splendor and pageantry and glory, don't we? We want to have an exciting, moving part to play in the drama of life."

Toward seven o'clock, the Fellowship of Isis members started to take their leave, the pub filled up with its Clonegal regulars, and Olivia and I began to say our goodbyes. In a lyrical mood, I recited some nostalgic lines by W. B. Yeats, and Olivia told me that Yeats had been a family friend of the Durdin-Robertsons and that she herself had had tea with him in his Dublin house in the

1930s. Sixty years later, she said, the great poet "came through" at a séance that she had attended in London. She was able to identify him by his "sonorous, chanting way of talking. . . . He gave the group a message—I'll never forget it. It was 'The Well and the Sword . . . no more . . . the trees have ears.' Then silence. . . . That was the message that came through."

"Speaking of great writers," I added, "shortly before he died, Jorge Luis Borges wrote a parable called 'The Gallic Goddess,' which concludes, 'We shall never hear the prayers of her worshipers, we shall never know her rites.' "

"Shortly before he died," Olivia remarked, "Borges *joined* the Fellowship of Isis! What happened was that a chap named Tom Mooney, who was presenting a radio program on Irish culture at the University of California at Santa Barbara—near where your President Reagan lives!—somehow started telling Borges about the Fellowship a few minutes before a meeting with the university chancellor. Borges was so interested in what Mooney was saying that he actually kept the chancellor waiting. He told Mooney that he and his Japanese lady friend wanted to join; Mooney told me; and I sent Borges and the lady their certificates."

"After five thousand years or so," I said, "Isis still seems to be alive and well at Clonegal Castle."

"She's *always* been here," Olivia asserted. "Evoë Isis! I think she stood aside to allow her divine son, Horus, to teach us. Then we turned away from her and had to learn from the Buddha and Jesus because we didn't want Mother. Now she's coming back, but I don't think she's coming back as Mother. I think she's coming back as girlfriend—as a companion, as a friend. You're looking for her, but you're not looking for a mother, are you? And I'm not looking for Daddy, I *have* Daddy—a very patriarchal God. I'm looking for boyfriend—as a companion, as a friend. You're looking for Isis and I'm looking for Osiris!"

5

ISIS AND OSIRIS:

A Conversation with

Robert S. Bianchi

*D*r. Robert S. Bianchi is currently a J. Clawson Mills Fellow at the Metropolitan Museum of Art in New York. Until recently, he was curator in the Department of Egyptian, Classical, and Ancient Middle Eastern Art at the Brooklyn Museum, where he focused primarily on the art and culture of Egypt during the Graeco-Roman period (332 B.C.–A.D. 323).

At his suggestion, I met Dr. Bianchi at the Explorers Club, a center dedicated to the advancement of scientific exploration of land, sea, the air, and space. Its members have included Admiral Peary, Theodore Roosevelt, Charles Lindbergh, Thor Heyerdahl, Sir Edmund Hillary, Tenzing Norgay, and John H. Glenn, Jr. Founded in 1904, the club has its headquarters in a six-story, Tudor-style townhouse on Manhattan's Upper East Side.

Dr. Bianchi and I met at the club in May 1992 and conversed in the Rare Books Room on the second floor, a stately and spacious area filled with bookcases containing, among other treasures, the twenty-four-volume *Description de l'Égypte* commissioned by Napoleon, with its incomparable engravings. It also contains paintings of an assortment of explorers, bas-relief panels, mullioned windows, and a carved oak refectory table in the center. All in all, the room was a conducive spot in which to reflect on Isis and Osiris and what happened to these gods after Alexander the Great conquered Egypt in 332 B.C.:

The concept of Isis as a mother goddess is one of great antiquity in Egypt, already attested to in the late Old King-

dom. But the *cult* of Isis—the idea of *the* Mother Goddess—
gained strength mainly in the Third Intermediate Period, about
1100 to 700 B.C. Numerous mother goddesses were worshiped
at that time—Hathor and Mut, among the most important—
but Isis, with her consort, Osiris, was somehow catapulted to
the top, so that by the time of the Thirtieth Dynasty in the
fourth century B.C., she was preeminent among the mother
goddesses.

This preeminence was coincident with the arrival of the
Greeks in Egypt. They were looking for an Egyptian deity that
could in some way be the counterpart of the very strong Ptolemaic queens. Now, native Egyptian Pharaonic women—and
I emphasize the word *Pharaonic*—had a greater degree of freedom and a better economic situation than did their Greek and
Roman equals. For example, Egyptian Pharaonic women
could control their own finances, and they could retain control
over real estate that they acquired before and after their marriages. Even women in the court of the fourth-century B.C.
Macedonian conquerors already had more freedom, in the
modern sense, than did the majority of Greek women. Think
of Olympias, the mother of Alexander the Great, who left
Macedonia in 331 B.C. and took up residence in Epirus, which
she ruled alone and with an iron fist for years. Arsinoe II, the
daughter of Ptolemy I, ruled the cities of Heraclea and Amas-
tris as her special domains. And Cleopatra VII, the last Macedonian ruler of Egypt (51–30 B.C.), was rooted in both of these
traditions and singlehandedly challenged the might of Rome.
And I think it is no coincidence that Cleopatra VII was, like
other Ptolemaic queens, associated with Isis. In fact, the decoration of the monumental rear wall of the so-called Temple of
Hathor at Dendera shows her worshiping not Hathor, but Isis
herself!

So when the Ptolemys came to Egypt, their women were
able to act very independently, and I think they found that
they could move about freely in society because the Egyptian
women could do so. So when one finds the rulers of the country asserting themselves through their female counterparts, one

naturally seeks a theological basis for that. And the goddess that best fit this political agenda was, of course, Isis. Neith was to become associated with Athena, Hathor with Aphrodite, and so on. But when you read Plutarch, you gain a sense that Isis was the one and only goddess of her stature. And then, because the Greeks controlled the Mediterranean to such a great extent, they exported the Isis religion.

If one looks at the Late Period Egyptian temples, one notices some extraordinary things. Even though the Temple of Hathor at Dendera, which was probably built in the late Ptolemaic–early Roman period, was ostensibly dedicated to Hathor, Isis was one of the major images on the outside. When you travel further south, Isis is the deity of Philae—and she remained so. And at the Dendur Temple, which was built under the reign of Augustus (c. 30 B.C.) and which is now in the Metropolitan Museum of Art, you'll notice that at some time, perhaps in the early Christian period, the temple was converted into a church. But it was originally a temple to Isis—regardless of what anybody says to the contrary. One reads in the literature that it's a temple to two brothers, Pedesi and Pihor, who reportedly drowned in the Nile; but in fact it's an Isis temple in which the goddess rented rooms, so to speak, to these two guys.

Some maintain that the Christians, for liturgical reasons, needed another lateral axis, and the only way to put in the door was to disfigure Isis on what is now the temple's north wall, so her arm was truncated. But after the door was made, they cut another arm, raised up in the air. If you look closely, you'll observe that Isis has two arms extending out of one armpit. Although this was only a pagan temple, the deity was still so powerful that even the Christians who *converted* the temple must have said, "Oops, we ritually mutilated the goddess, so we've got to put her back together whole." So I think she had this enormous hold on the early Christian mind.

I once wrote an article in which I indicated, very blithely from an academic vantage point, that the Christian image of the Madonna nursing the Christ Child was indebted to Isis nursing Horus. I stated that as a matter of academic fact. Several people read the article and took umbrage at what I'd said because they thought I had insulted or somehow demeaned the Christ Child and the Virgin Mary. All I had done was to indicate that from an academic point of view, there was this parallel—that Isis and Horus are the model on which Christian iconography is built. Certainly by the time of Christ, the Osiris legend was in great circulation. And if you want to make a comparative-religion case there, I think you could do that too. I tried to factor out religious conviction on the one hand and academic rationalism on the other, and I agree that the two don't necessarily intersect. But a religious prejudice should not prevent you from exploring the possibility.

When you come to the Hellenistic period, the Isis cult began with free-enterprising individuals who realized that they might be able to make a buck. Without any official, royal, or ecclesiastical support, they went to a place like Delos and announced, "I'm an Egyptian, Isis is cool, sign up!" This may sound like TV evangelism, but I think that that's the way it spread. And then it became such a hot-ticket item that everybody wanted to get into it, and thus the cult grew. The $64,000 question is, what was it about this cult that was so magnetic that it captured mankind and womankind for almost three hundred years? Except for who knows what vagaries, we in the West might today be Isis devotees instead of Jews, Christians, or Muslims. She must have satisfied a very real, physical need that the other cults of the time didn't. And this becomes a very interesting question from a feminist point of view, because one has to try to explain why, in those male-oriented societies, this female-dominated religion became so entrenched and popular. This is a woman, after all, not Mithras or Christ, who is the salvation not only of women but of so many men.

People living during the Roman Empire were looking for a way of overcoming fate and were engaged in a quest for salvation. The story of the martyred Osiris with a beautiful and caring wife who caused his resurrection must have moved the people. The Roman state religion, after all, was a very cold, noncharismatic worship. You sacrificed a bull and you went home. There wasn't much ecstasy there, and Isis filled that void. We're told that when the Tiber River froze, the priests of Isis ordered the devotees to dig a hole and jump three times into the ice, with great risk of life—and this, remember, was a dedication to an abstract cause, not to the state.

Now, concerning Osiris: he may have been the consort of Isis in Pharaonic times. But either Ptolemy I or Ptolemy II concocted a hybrid god they called Serapis, who combined the characteristics of Osiris on the one hand and of Hades on the other. The result was an Egyptian theological concept outfitted in Greek clothes. The Egyptians, naturally, couldn't relate to this at all, while the Greeks in Egypt merely paid lip service to the cult.

Then, when the cult got exported, Serapis always appeared with Isis—though he was never called her husband; her husband was always Osiris. So you got this strange ménage à trois: Isis was always posturing in public with Serapis (thanks to the Ptolemys), but everybody knew her real consort was Osiris. And that's why a lot of the Egyptian cults in the Mediterranean were situated in what we now call Serapis temples.

One of the largest pagan temples I've ever seen is in the city of Pergamum in Turkey. The floor of this temple spans the confluence of two rivers that flow through the center of the city, so in ancient times, when these two rivers overflowed, they reenacted the flooding of the Nile! But even though Isis played a very significant role in the temple, it was called the Serapeum. In Pompeii, on the other hand, you could find a Temple of Isis. But those were the only two alternatives. Outside Egypt, you almost never found a Temple of Osiris. There was an Iseum or a Serapeum, and that was it.

What can we make of Isis and Osiris from the perspective of Ptolemaic Egypt? Looking back is easy. The West has had the prejudice that the ancient Egyptians restarted the clock or calendar at one every time there was a new king, and therefore the West has considered that Egypt never had a linear view of history but had a cyclical one. Acceptance of that theory, however, denies the Egyptians a historic perspective, an ability to look back over time. We're learning today that the Egyptians had an incredible historic sense—though it may not have been ours—and when appropriate, they could reach back two to three thousand years.

One example: During his reign (c. 1391–1353 B.C.), Amenhotep III celebrated a Sed, or Jubilee, Festival. And the contemporary texts of that time tell us that Amenhotep went back to try to find out how the festival was originally celebrated. From his reign we have found fragments of slate palettes, something that no longer existed after Egypt was unified, around 3000 B.C. So when one comes across one of these palettes inscribed with the name of Amenhotep, it indicates that his was no idle boast. When he said that he was going to go back to the origin, he knew where to go to look.

Similarly, from the vantage point of the Ptolemaic period, if I wanted to, I could look back to the dawn of Egyptian civilization and study the Isis cult. I *guarantee* I could do that. If I were one of the elite priests during the Ptolemaic period and somebody asked what happened a millennium ago, I believe I would know where to look for the answer; and depending on how complete or incomplete the record was, I could give you the answer.

The reason that the records didn't come down from that period is that the majority of Egypt's population converted to Christianity, and the language changed from hieroglyphs to Coptic. Shortly thereafter, the country was conquered by the Arabs. During the Middle Ages, the Arabs figured there might be a fifth column in Egypt in the guise of the Christians who were there, and the persecution of the Christians began, probably as a result of the Crusades.

With regard to all this, let me describe to you one of the most poignant episodes I know of. There's an inscription in the Temple of Philae, dating to the fourth century A.D., which in everybody's estimation is the last datable hieroglyphic inscription ever. So my fantasy has been to go back in time to that last group of priests who knew the hieroglyphs, and then see the guy who carved that last hieroglyph. . . . And when he died, no one could figure out what it said.

Right from the beginning, the Egyptian language and the hieroglyphs were the same. But the ancient Egyptians also believed that hieroglyphic signs were charged with representing the images that were *there*—which is to say, the signs could come to life. That's why in some of the Pyramid Texts the animal signs were intentionally truncated, lest the animals come back and kill the deceased king in his tomb. If a lion was drawn as forepart and hindpart, with a big chunk missing in the middle, the sign would be recognizable for its phonetic value and meaning, but the lion couldn't materialize and devour the king!

So I think we have to try to understand that the ancient Egyptian language was a substitute for reality—and I think they actually believed that—because any spell written in hieroglyphs was the most efficacious thing one could make. The word was so powerful because the word was an image. Every picture was potentially animate—which is a pretty extraordinary notion right there! So once you wrote something down, it had the power of jumping off the wall and coming to life. A kind of sympathetic magic.

But those who call the ancient Egyptians simple and childlike do not understand the profundity of the concept or the magnitude of the intellect that created pictographic writing at the dawn of history—that one man, as Henry Fisher recently argued, actually invented the hieroglyphic system of writing. Others argue that it might have been a committee, but everybody agrees that it was a coterie that transmitted the pictographic system and kept it to themselves for three thousand years. Egyptologists are of the opinion that less than 5 percent of the ancient population left us the material remains we now consider "Egyptian." So we don't know how 95 or even 97 percent of the people really lived.

Now, once you're in this very closed, elitist environment, knowledge is passed down in a secret and guarded way, which may have given rise to the Roman commentators' view of

Egypt as a mystical society, a society in which one had to pass through initiations in order to be privy to the information. And that may have been interpreted in the Middle Ages and later, especially by the Masons, to mean that admission is *via* initiation. The initiation may be a Western rationalization for what occurred when you were just born into the system. In Egypt, knowledge was the key to social position and wealth, and if you kept knowledge away from everybody, you were ensuring your economic and social position. I definitely believe the Egyptians were doing that. And that was one of the reasons society was able to stay unchanged for so long. They had an elite guarding everything.

But this elite didn't envisage that with the change of government and religion, their language would one day die out. That's why I try to imagine the genius who invented the language around 3000 B.C., and then try to imagine and empathize with that last priest who carved that last hieroglyph in the fourth century A.D. The oral tradition continued, of course, for a couple of hundred years or so . . . until one day, some guy in the Isis cult might have asked, "How do you do this?" And the priestess might have said, "God, I forget!" And there was nowhere to go to look it up.

In my opinion, the Plutarch story is one telling of the story of Isis, seen through the temperament and eyes and agenda of the author. It's not pure. That tradition was able to survive the death of the hieroglyphs because Westerners were never unable to read Greek and Latin. From the time Greek and Latin were written until the present day, anybody who has been educated has been able to read them—as opposed to Egyptian, which, after the fourth century, no one could read.

After the hieroglyphics died, we have an imperfectly understood oral tradition in Egypt and an altered or modified version in Plutarch, which, however imperfect, was transmitted by the people living in Egypt. But when the Greeks and Egyptians started to talk to one another, the confusion was rampant. And then the baggage of mythology about Egypt that built up in the Middle Ages also added to the way people interpreted Plutarch. By that time, you've got Egypt filtered through so many lenses that you're not seeing the Pharaonic period anymore.

I want to separate *conviction* from intellectual *speculation*. From the point of view of religious conviction, I firmly believe that an oral tradition might be able to span five thousand years. From a rational, academic point of view, however, I believe that if you asked the people in today's Isis cults to trace their cults back in time, you'd reach a point before which they didn't exist. And because you could demonstrate that there was a rupture in that family tree, you would not easily convince me of the oral tradition that we're talking about.

Now, if you ask me about something like Mozart's *The Magic Flute*—well, that is an interesting case. People who have studied the opera's libretto have discovered that the names of certain characters, like Papageno, can be broken down—or so it's thought—into their ancient Egyptian components. For instance, the name Papageno means "the bird catcher," and that's what the character is in the opera. So what tradition was alive that enabled the librettist to name the characters for the roles they played? How could that have been known when the translation of the hieroglyphs was still down the road? I'm not qualified to answer that question, but it is worth thinking about.

6

THE PEOPLE OF
THE FAITH:

The Ammonite Foundation

To preserve their anonymity, Her Grace Sekhmet Montu, her husband, Neb Ptah Hotep, and their son, Neb Heru, have requested that no photograph of them be included here.

"*T*here's a Holy Family that is living today in Cairo, Egypt," a member of the Fellowship of Isis informed me discreetly during my stay at Clonegal Castle. "They are Ammonites, and they're secretly practicing the ancient Egyptian religion." I was told that the family consisted of a woman, referred to as Her Grace Sekhmet Montu, who was said to be the spiritual leader of the Ammonites; her husband, Ptah Hotep; and their then nine-year-old son, known as Neb ("Lord" or "His Excellency") Heru.

"Heru is the word for Horus," I said incredulously to my informant.

"That's right. It's said that he is the god-being incarnate."

An entry in the *Isian News*, contributed by Sekhmet Montu herself, amplified this remark.

The Lotus Throne of Pharaoh is now occupied by two beings, namely myself and Neb Heru. The throne has always belonged to Neb Heru, but on August 21, 1989, both He and I physically ascended the throne. This establishes the beginning of the equality of masculine and feminine powers in the world in the new era. . . . At times I find it hard to grasp that prophecies really do come true, even when I see it happen. I hope it is to be that the Old Ways will return to the lands of Egypt, not only for my people but for all those who might find security and contentment within

Note: The names of the gods Isis, Osiris, and Horus are Greek renderings of the Egyptian Auset, Ausar, and Heru, respectively. In this chapter I have followed the Ammonite Foundation's practice of referring to the Egyptian forms of the gods, or *neters*, providing, when appropriate, the more familiar Greek names in parentheses.

the Old Ways, be these people 10 or 10 million. It will be. The seed is planted and sprouts. Time will bear the fruit of our efforts.

Who were these people claiming a lineage of several thousand years, and who was this family with its child of Hope (Horus) waiting to save the world? Was it imaginable that the story of Isis and Osiris was being played out once again in some unfathomable way?

I wanted to find out, but was informed that the Ammonites had lived in hiding throughout the Middle East for centuries, had guarded their privacy in fear of persecution, and had so far rejected any attempts to dig up information about themselves and their beliefs. Now, however, there was a movement toward the outside world. So through the good offices of Olivia Robertson, who was in correspondence with Sekhmet Montu, and because—so I was told—Her Grace had liked a book I had written, *The Search for Omm Sety*, about a remarkable twentieth-century English-Egyptian priestess of Isis, I was invited to pay a visit to the spiritual leader of the Ammonite Foundation in Cairo. "We will be happy," a letter from the foundation informed me, "to do what we can to help and assist your understanding of our branch of the Faith, but bear in mind, our situation here is at best dicey, and the local religion very intolerant at best. So mum's the word!"

Eight months went by before I was able to travel to Cairo. I got there one morning at the end of May 1990, and it was already ninety-eight degrees when I walked out of the plane into the blinding light of the day. I checked into my hotel at noon and proceeded to follow the instructions given to me in a letter by an Ammonite royal scribe named Senmut. I had been told to call a certain telephone number, ask for a Dr. X or a Dr. Y, and leave both my own and my hotel's name and my room number with a man named Z, who had a phone in his shop. I was also advised to speak slowly and clearly because Z's English was poor, then wait for a return call. So I phoned Mr. Z and asked for Dr. X or Dr. Y. I repeated my name and number several times, hung up, and waited.

About an hour later I received a call from a man speaking hesitant, accented English. He welcomed me to Cairo and told me to take a cab to a certain restaurant in a particular section of the city, get out, and walk three or four blocks east toward a certain street, where I would be recognized and guided to Her Grace's residence. I had been informed beforehand that I would never be allowed to visit her without an escort.

When I went outside it had reached 104 degrees, and there seemed to be at least 104 taxis lingering in the street. It was coming on to summer, just months after the Gulf war, and there were few tourists around.

Being inside a cab that afternoon was like being in the Eastern Desert, with the added spectacle of gaggles of chaotically driven cars weaving in, out, through, and around everywhere, all incessantly honking like demented geese. So when the taxi arrived at my destination about fifteen minutes ahead of schedule—in spite of the traffic—I decided to take advantage of my flagging and disoriented state to tarry awhile and look around. In this working-class neighborhood there was a lot to see.

On every building hung a profusion of brilliantly colored wash on clotheslines—blue, red, maroon, pink, and yellow garments, dazzling and unmoving in the stagnant air. Men in djellabas and fezzes smoked water pipes and played dominoes in outdoor cafés. Women in dark robes walked slowly with their children. Scrawny cats curled up in any available patch of shade. I passed by shops selling pastry, nuts, fruit, shoes, even plastic restaurant chairs—hundreds of white chairs sitting on top of each other in groups of tens. In a seven-by-three-foot hole in a wall, I saw a tailor squeezed over a sewing machine, mending curtains. And I stood for a couple of minutes and stared in amazement at the jumble of merchandise all squashed together in the window of one small store: coffee cups, picture frames, hydraulic jacks, tripods, beach balls, toothpaste, insect repellant, bicycle bells, plastic dolls, hair-styling sets, packages of British cigarettes, and telephone receivers. The whole world in one window!

When I crossed the street, someone was heading toward me—a tall, thin, light-skinned man in his mid-thirties, with a shaved head, high cheekbones, and a handlebar mustache, wearing a white cotton robe, a black cummerbund, and leather sandals. The sign of Ra, ☉, was tattooed on his forehead. He bowed slightly and, without saying anything, motioned me to follow him as he walked with graceful steps down a side street. We entered one of the twenty-five or so crumbling houses and mounted several flights of stairs. The man in white knocked on a peeling door, and a woman opened it. Fair-skinned, blue-eyed, in her early forties, she was wearing two white scarves—one under her neck, the other over her head, held in place by a flat white hat—a white blouse, and a dark apron covering a blue skirt. A gold chain was linked from her right nostril to her right ear—a sign of Ammonite priesthood. On her face and hands she bore several symbolic marks and tattoos.

"Hi, I hope you didn't have too much trouble getting here," she said to me in perfect, Southwest-inflected American English.

As I started to shake her hand, she quickly stepped back and shook her head, making it clear that she was not to be touched. Then she pointed to the curious little boy standing just behind her, a smiling, pale, undissembling nine-year-old with a shaved head (except for a braided sidelock on the right side, called an *antet*). He was wearing thick-lensed glasses that emphasized his slightly crossed left eye—the result of cholera—as well as a brown cotton shirt, Mickey Mouse trousers, and white sneakers.

"This," she said, "is my son."

"You're all the way from United States?" he asked me awkwardly in a charming, bell-like voice.

"All the way."

"Well, come *in!*" he commanded with a giggle.

His mother now said something to him in a serious tone in a language I did not recognize. Led by her child, I walked through the hallway of this faded but pleasant four-room apartment into a narrow sitting room with a marble tile floor, which served as a living room. An ancient Egyptian calendar with the New Year beginning on June 20 and a painting of a red lotus hung on one of the walls, painted orange, beige, dark green, and mustard brown, and two canaries and a finch chirped and jumped about overhead in a hanging cage. The little boy sat down next to me on a long couch with blue cushions, and his mother and the man in white sat across from us on two chairs separated by a table with some roses and a plant on it. The radio music and bustling sounds of the Cairo streets came through the open, curtained windows, as did the heat of the day. The man in white offered me a bottle of cold Egyptian beer, which I gratefully accepted.

"Do you know who we are?" the woman asked me.

"Only that in the Bible it says that the Midianites and the Ammonites—"

"Yes," she interrupted, "in *your* Book it's claimed that the Israelites wiped out the Ammonites thousands of years ago. But here we are!" She smiled. "We've been in hiding a *long* time," she added, "because we knew that the Jews and the Arabs, among others, would try to commit genocide against us, and we weren't that many people. We've been a hidden community; and it's only now, in the new era, that our prophecies have said that there would be true seekers in the West and other places wishing to return to the House of *Neters*, to the gods we know and worship. So we—the Sau Council and I—decided to let you come and talk to some of us. Though most of our people aren't ready to come out; it would be genocide if they did so."

At this point, the man in white emphasized something to the woman in another language.

"This is my husband," she told me. "And although he understands a little English, he doesn't really speak it."

"What language is he speaking?" I asked.

"Pars-nawab. It's basically Farsi, with some hieroglyphic words mixed in, and we speak it because we've lived with the Iranians a long time. My husband is saying that we must ask you to refer to us in your book by our priestly Ammonite names— Sekhmet Montu, Ptah Hotep, Heru or Heru Khuti, which means Horus of the Double Horizon—and not by the Arabic names we're known by here in Cairo. The three of us were already imprisoned in another Middle Eastern country—I won't say which one—because they found out who we were, and if it hadn't been for constant prayer and a lot of wisdom in dealing with the people who imprisoned us, we would have been killed. So what name I use here is not important to your book."

Over the next three hours, as Heru carefully investigated my cassette recorder, Sekhmet Montu explained to me

- that the Ammonite Foundation (more accurately, the Foundation of Ammun-Ra) was started, as it had been prophesied it would be, after the downfall of the reign of the "heretic" Akhenaten, by the ancient Egyptian boy-king Tutankhamon in order to protect the sacred Book of the Faith from corruption.

- that since it had been foretold that Egypt would one day fall, about ten thousand People of the Faith, as the Ammonites called themselves, made an exodus by royal decree during the reign of Rameses II, taking the Book with them, joining one of the Egyptian army garrisons, and establishing settlements in Kadesh, Petra, and Rabbath-Ammon, the site of present-day Amman.

- that contrary to the beliefs of certain scholars, the Ammonites were and are not Arabs.

- that the Ammonites represent the true branch of the ancient Egyptian religion, but that Egyptologists, having followed the "famous part of the tree," believed that the entire tree had died during the Ptolemaic era and had therefore neglected to see what is still living. This intentional act of disappearance was made to protect the 27,000 or so Ammonite people living today.

- that the Ammonites have for thousands of years been a nomadic people, traveling with their horses, camels, and black tents through Afghanistan, Pakistan, Iran, Iraq, and Jordan, concealing their faith and working mostly in leather and gold and selling vegetables and sheep. Sekhmet Montu told me that certain tribes in Iraq and Iran were "*our* people," and that she herself had made the trip from Basra to Afghanistan and back several times.

- that many thousands of Ammonites had been living and practicing their faith in secret throughout all the wars in the Middle East and that some were in fact still suffering massive extermination at the time of our conversation. A lot of Ammonite resources were being used to get them out of their excruciating circumstances, but because they were refugees without legal papers or with only World Service Authority passports, they were extremely difficult to assist.

• that the several hundred Ammonites now living in Egypt are there not as Egyptian citizens but as foreigners who neither proselytize nor talk to anyone about their faith. "Some of the people here know I perform magic and healing," Sekhmet Montu remarked. "I do it for some of them, but they don't know who I am."

• that except for some Ma'i/Zoroastrian intermarriages, Ammonites almost always marry within the faith. If they do choose to marry outside the group, however—or even if they just wish to leave for whatever reason—they are free to do so, as long as they promise to reveal nothing about the community to the outside world.

• that Sekhmet Montu's husband was born in the desert, the Wadi Rum in Jordan; and that she was born in Lebanon, though her origins remain somewhat obscure, by design.

• that though she has to search for words now and then, she speaks English like a native American because she was sent to the States, "for a definite reason." She lived there for a number of years with a family who didn't know that she was an Ammonite, then returned to the Middle East, in 1982.

• that her husband was severely injured in a bomb explosion

"during a Middle Eastern war" and because of extensive injuries had to have wires placed in his arms and legs. He developed epilepsy and was therefore forced to leave his tribe and adopt a sedentary life.

- that she and her husband have both taken a vow of poverty, and that he supports the family with a job that pays $100 a month.

- that the Ammonites have strict dietary and dress codes and moral and community laws: "The style of dress is optional but must not show any lines or form or bear any decoration which is conducive of showing or accenting what is underneath"; "All seafood and/or water-borne foods are forbidden in their entirety"; "Keep chaste and pure in body, soul, and spirit, save only your bewedded spouse, and then only after marriage even until death and after."

- that Ammonites are bound by the Forty-two Laws of the Saints, commonly known as the Negative Confessions from the *Egyptian Book of the Dead.* One is supposed to proclaim these in the Hall of Judgment after one's death, stating that one has not "ill-treated animals," "sought to deceive by saying 'I know that which is not yet,'" "been lazy," "tolerated the sight of evil," "warped the Scales of Justice," "stopped loving all things," "stolen from the earth nor the dead it keeps," "diminished the food of the earth," etc. "If you followed the Forty-two Laws," Sekhmet Montu stated, "you wouldn't need environmental conferences or peace movements or even governments."

- that the Ammonite priests and priestesses, as the servants

of the *neters* on earth, keep the tribe together and finan-
cially support their temples by themselves.

- that as spiritual leader and divine link, Sekhmet Montu is
the emanation through divination of the gods Auset and
Ausar, and that her husband, a priest, has as his *neter* patron the god Anpu (Anubis).

- that her patron deity is the lion-headed Goddess Sekhmet,
consort of the God Ptah, who is called "the Destroyer"
because she "prods us to change and grow and search into
the unknown, encouraging curiosity, manifesting the anti-
force of the physical stability within us, without which we
would fall into the darkness of ourselves."

- that a picture of Her Grace Sekhmet Montu hangs above
the doors of Ammonite households.

- that there are two secret Ammonite advisory and admin-
istrative bodies, each made up of twenty-one men and
twenty-one women, who are the high priests and priestesses of all the temples. These are called the Sa and Sau
Councils, and communicate with each other by mail,
phone, and special couriers. There is a material leader,
known as the Suten Bat, or king, and a "spiritual" leader—
chosen by the Sau Council and the Suten Bat—known as
the Per-āa, the Great House.

- that Sekhmet Montu fulfilled the twelve requirements—
physical, soulful, spiritual, and hidden, including blood
type, choice of patron, life regressions, approach to the

Book—to qualify for the position of the Great House, or Pharaoh.

• and that it was Her Grace Sekhmet Montu who nine years ago gave birth to the son (the Heru god-being incarnate) who ascended the Lotus Throne with her on August 21, 1989, in front of an audience of one thousand Ammonites. He was "the Divine Son of Auset," I was told, and was at that moment sitting next to me on a couch in this apartment here in the heart of Cairo.

"Auset and Ausar are my spiritual mother and father," Sekhmet Montu said to me when I returned to see her the next morning. At her side was her husband, Ptah Hotep, who acted as our chaperon and occasionally spoke to her in Pars-nawab when he thought she might emphasize or explain something to me more fully.

"When Auset and Ausar came here," she continued in a mesmerizing but at the same time matter-of-fact manner, "they taught us how to worship, as well as the rudiments of civilization—how to cultivate land, grow crops, write, institute community laws. They banished cannibalism and did away with the inequality of the sexes, and they themselves gave us the Forty-two Laws, the prayers, and the basic principles of the Book, which is the ultimate expression of God Force. They were here for about fifty years, but we didn't start counting ourselves as followers until the death of Ausar, and the date of his ascension into the otherworld marks the first day of the Ammonite calendar—12,453 years ago from this June 21, 1991!

"Later, though, there was a period during which the teachings were followed in a very lax manner, so they were lost to us for a time. And this was the period when the Goddess Sekhmet

Montu—Avenger of All Wrongs, Lioness, and Eye of the Divine Mother and Father—came to destroy all mankind in one of her bloody rampages.

"Then, in the reign of the Pharaoh you call Khufu, there was a man named Heru-ta-ta-fu, which means 'the Giver of His Own Hope,' who appeared seemingly out of nowhere. No one knew where he was from, but he spoke all the dialects of all the nomes [districts] of Egypt, and he could read and write better than any scribe of that day. 'I am Egyptian' was all he would answer to those asking where he was born. He knew all the prayers, hymns, and ceremonies, and he knew by heart all the sacred books of the day—the *Book of Tahuti*, the *Book of Gates*, and the *Book of the Gods*. He knew all the sacred places of pilgrimage, even to describing the marks on their walls—though no one could remember ever having seen him in those places.

"He was a pious and honest man, and he worked himself up to the position of inspector of temples. In the third year of his duties he went to the Temple of Neb Ptah in Sakkara, having come from the Sanctuary of Ammun in Wast [Luxor], and while praying in the shrine there he heard a voice telling him to go into the inner sanctum and look at the feet of the great God Tahuti, where he would discover something important. So he did, and found a book unlike any other, written upon metal plates that glowed with light! He took the Book to the Pharaoh, who ordered a copy to be made from the plates. Heru-ta-ta-fu never left the Book during the copying, and when he was certain that each letter and sign was exact, he suddenly turned to the Book and said, 'Is the copy true and correct?' From which a voice replied, 'It is, come home.' The Book enlarged itself, and suddenly both it and Heru-ta-ta-fu vanished in a flash of blue-white light, and a voice proclaimed, 'I am the Living Word, the Book called *Per-em-Hru-Em-Akhet-Ammun-Ra,* and all shall eventually come to know me!' The Book disappeared into a secret chamber, and that original Book exists—it's not where anyone but a few of us can find it. But we've had *copies* of the Book ever since, which we've tried to keep as close to the original as is humanly possible."

It was not the first nor the last time during our conversations that I would look at Sekhmet Montu with an expression of wonder, incredulity, bewilderment, and skepticism. But if God had written the Torah with His finger, and if the Koran was revealed by God to the Prophet Muhammad, why mightn't the *Per-em-Hru-Em-Akhet-Ammun-Ra* have been delivered to the priest Heru-ta-ta-fu?

Noticing the hesitancy of my response, Sekmet Montu calmly remarked, "We don't see things as myths. We *believe* that they all happened. They may not have happened *physically*—though we believe they did—but even if they didn't, they did happen in principle throughout mankind as a whole."

"What does the Book consist of?" I asked.

"The *Per-em-Hru,* or the *Book of the Dead,*" Sekhmet Montu told me, "is used for the transition into and passage through the Hall of Judgment." She added, "About 80 percent of this material can be found, in a different order, in E. A. Wallis Budge's famous version of the *Egyptian Book of the Dead.* But the second part of the Book—the *Akhet-Ammun-Ra, The Horizon of Ammun-Ra*—wasn't buried with the dead, and it contains what you need to know while alive on the earth and explains how to worship and understand how the principles of *neters* manifest in the universe. . . . So these two parts make up the Book."

"And what does the Book sound like?" I asked.

"We all read and speak the Medu [hieroglyphics]," Sekhmet Montu told me. "I use it for prayers and ceremonies or when addressing the Sau Council. And just like any language, the spoken Medu has different dialects. The one I chose is from the Delta. My son learned the Medu when he was five, and now he reads and speaks it. Don't you, Heru?"

"A *very* little," he said, looking a bit sheepish.

"He also speaks Pars-nawab, Arabic, and a little English," his mother added.

"A little," Heru agreed with a smile. "My mother teaches me at home."

"Until recently," she informed me, "it was the mothers and women in our tribes who read and wrote out the Book; our men memorized it. Our priests, however, both male and female, read it, and my husband helped me in my studies. And now we are teaching all the children to read and write as well. Maybe Heru would read you something so that you can hear the Medu."

The boy went over to his mother, who gave him three pages containing the Twelve Laws of Ammun-Ra, written out by Sekhmet Montu in the Medu, the Nawab (its transliteration), and English. Heru came back to the couch, sat down next to me, and slowly recited the laws in Medu as I looked over his shoulder to follow the English translation at the bottom of each line.

I.

Su-kheperu   ānkh
Create   life

2.

Merr-t   ānkh
Love   life

3.

S-renp   ānkh
Redeem   life

4.

S-kheperu saá-t kheft ānkh
Create knowledge for life

5.

Pesesh merr-t neth ānkh
Share love of life

6.

S-nekhen ānkh nebu
Redeem all life

7.

S-khen maāt
Keep truth

8.

Merr-t maāt
Love truth

9.

Pesesh maāt
Share truth

10.

S-kheper ā er āb ānkh
Create a more pure life

11.

S-kheper ā er āb merr-t
Create a more pure love

12.

S-kheper ā er āb maāt
Create a more pure truth

"I will repeat for you what my husband told me many years ago," Sekhmet Montu said to me. "I will repeat the words exactly as he said them to me. 'When I was a child,' he said, 'I fell in love with words and God and sacred places on hearing my grandfather proclaim in the Medu, "O Ra! I am born each day upon Your rising; beautiful are Your creations, wondrous is all You have made!" My heart overflowed at the *sound* of those words that he spoke on the plains of Giza, just as the sun was setting behind the pyramids, and then later, once again, on the Holy Mountain of Creation, Mount Sinai, but this time with the sun *rising* behind the mountain. I remember I asked my grandfather why he repeated the same prayer at the setting and the rising of the sun. He said, "As it was the setting which caused the rising, I honor it, too, for the Dark raises up the Light, and the Light here on this mountain raises up the Dark of Creation for all to perceive, and the prayer makes one humble before the majesty of God!"

" 'Now, my conversation with my grandfather was held in Medu, just as the prayer he spoke was. When I studied to be a priest years later, the Medu again moved upon my heart like a wave, and I thanked God for that beautiful moment with my grandfather when I felt that the world was sacred and the words in Medu and the Book were sacred, and that the earth was the body of the God Geb!' "

"I didn't realize that Mount Sinai, where Moses received the Ten Commandments, was also sacred to the Ammonites," I remarked to Sekhmet Montu.

"It's where Nut, Goddess of the Sky, gave birth to Ausar, Auset, Setekh [Set], Nebt Het [Nephthys], and Heru, which is why we call it the Mount of Creation. It's also the place where the Goddess Sekhmet Montu first stepped on the earth when she came to destroy the people at the command of her father, Ra. We call it the Mountain of Sunrise. . . . But speaking of Mount Sinai," Sekhmet Montu suddenly remarked, "I hope you don't mind my asking if you are Jewish."

"I am."

"I thought you were," she said, "and it's strange, because you're the first Jewish person who has been anywhere near our people."

"Are Jews forbidden?"

"There's something within you *personally* that the Sau Council likes, or else I wouldn't be here with you now."

"Why?"

"Because of the differences of our philosophies. That's why we live in the desert, so we don't have to deal with them."

"The people or the philosophies?"

"First, we think that a polytheistic monotheism is the most

accurate, expressive, and understandable method of worship, and that one should avoid the popular belief of concentrating on 'the One' and instead pay closer attention to 'the All.' And we interpret *your* God, the one God of the Judeo-Christian-Muslim tradition generally, as Setekh, the God of Negativity.

"In the story of creation that we believe in," Sekhmet Montu continued, "all the gods emerged with their specific principles, but they were still evolving. God began in unawareness, then evolved to a point of awareness that we can't possibly comprehend. During the time that the gods were all evolving, however, they discarded the negativity within themselves, which was generated by the very creation itself, and a composite of all the negativity was made into another *neter* in order to provide for another perspective and awareness. This is the *neter* we call Setekh. He *is* One. He's the one with all the negativity the other gods put into him. But we don't see him as *completely* negative, either. Setekh is also a helpful god. Before the dismemberment of Ausar, he was the Great Teacher and was greatly revered in Egypt. And there are still people among us who worship him. He is One—but he is not the *only* One!

"Then your people put all this stuff on our heads about how they had to build the pyramids and how they were slaves here. And our people resent that, because they didn't *do* that. Your people were kicked out of Saudi Arabia and came into Egypt. They were hungry; we gave them bread, clothing, housing, work—for these are the basic moral principles that we practice. Then they left Egypt and made a problem for us. This is how we see it. But we don't know why. And we're not happy about it. And because they did it, we leave them alone.

"Your Bible says that we fought along with the Canaanites and Moabites against your people. So we knew that we could be in a lot of trouble, because the fundamentalists among your people thought they'd already wiped us out, and if they found out that they hadn't gotten all of us, they might try and get us *now!* And we're not that many people—there are only about twenty-seven thousand of us. We were afraid that the fundamentalist Jews, and the fundamentalist Muslims, might attack us. So we have stayed hidden. But if there was ever a situation when your people were willing to engage in a battle of minds instead of try-ing to kill off the physical manifestations, we could perhaps live in peace."

"Well, here I am!" I remarked. "But I have to say that your definition of the one God is not mine at all, since what I think of as 'the One' is what you call 'the All.' My concept of Judaism has nothing to do with and rejects the ancient biblical injunctions to kill men, women, and male children. In fact, I personally wish all of you life, health, and strength!"

"Regardless of what you think of your God, and regardless of what we think of him," Sekhmet Montu replied, "the God of Resurrection is *your* Father and *my* Father, and we see him as Au-sar. And you're always welcome in his house, any time, any place. Because he's the Father of everyone; there's no one who should be left out. Everyone will eventually come home to the house of their Father. Do you see?"

Ptah Hotep whispered something to his wife while looking at me. She said, "My husband had an audience with Ausar last night, and Ausar said you were to have this today."

Ptah Hotep stood up and presented me with a four-inch-high, white, green, and gold metal statuette of the God Ausar, crowned and with his crook and flail. Ptah Hotep and his wife buy these figurines in the market, rework them, paint them, then use them in their worship. He spoke to me in a gentle voice, and Sekhmet Montu translated his words.

"My husband says, Ausar is the Father of you and of him.

Maybe brothers fight, but they still live in the same house. My husband is in the service of the God Anpu [Anubis]. Because he is, he says it's up to him at least to show you the path as he sees it. He also says, 'The one you call *your* Father [Setekh] is the brother of the one we call *our* Father [Ausar]. We both come from the same place. We're both from one family.' "

As I started gathering up my belongings, Sekhmet Montu said, "Before you leave for the day, I just want you to understand that we believe in being direct, and we're being direct with you. We don't talk behind people's backs. If you were a Christian, we'd say what differences we have with *that* tradition. Olivia Robertson, whom we think of as our older sister and whom I've been corresponding with for three years, takes the good from everything and focuses on that. *We* recognize the good within everything, but we let it be known from the start what the differences are between us and another person. So that there are no misunderstandings later.

"You see, we too have been victims of discrimination, genocide, and we've had our own exile—the same things you've been through. So we can understand the Jewish people and their sufferings. Therefore, we should at least be able to tolerate each other. It's wrong to persecute *anyone*."

During my conversations with Sekhmet Montu, Heru had sat next to me playing with a Ping-Pong ball or with a ridged straw, bending it up and down for extended periods with great interest. Occasionally, he asked me if he could examine my cassette recorder, which he did gently but intently. So at the end of my second visit, I mentioned to Sekhmet Montu that I would like to buy Heru a Walkman as a gift, and Heru, who had only a little, beat-up phonograph, was overjoyed at the prospect. A lively discussion in Pars-nawab between mother and son ensued, and it was finally suggested that I meet both of them the next morning at Midan el-Tahrir (Liberation Square) and we could then walk to three or four shops that sold Walkmans.

All of Cairo's main traffic arteries meet at Midan el-Tahrir, which is also the home of the Ministry of Foreign Affairs, the National Assembly, the Egyptian Museum, and the American University. I had been told to meet Sekhmet Montu and Heru in front of the American University, but I was arriving from the opposite direction and it took me about fifteen minutes just to navigate through streams of honking cars and scores of over-loaded, swaying trams coming at me from everywhere, so I was late for my appointment. From a distance, I could easily make out mother and son, dressed much as they had been the past two days, waiting on the street, with masses of people walking past them. As I approached, I noticed two Egyptian women in black robes stopping in front of the little boy, staring at him, and saying something to Sekhmet Montu.

"Don't worry," she assured me with a laugh when I apolo-gized for being late. "We had some uninvited visitors."

"What did they have to say?" I asked.

"The usual: 'Is that a boy or a girl? That's a *boy*? How? Why? Where are you from?' 'It's none of your business,' I told them in Arabic. I *always* say that, every time we go out. Heru's sidelock and shaved head are nothing to him, he's not affected by them. He's gotten to be a pretty tough little cracker! And when people get really hostile, I just speak English and disarm them, so they think I'm just one of those weird foreigners who worship the an-cient Egyptians! I guess it's funny, but if I ever went back to the West, my English would make people doubt me, while in Cairo it protects me.

"Some of the people here call us the White Nubians. Some confuse us for the Druse . . . and in fact, a long time ago we *were* all one group, and later branched off into two. They didn't have the Book, but they had some of the prayers and basic teachings and still live by them. And then there's a town on the Red Sea whose inhabitants don't speak or look Arabic, and they won't carry papers. They're cordoned off. The soldiers won't let anybody in or out . . . and I'm sure they're remnants of our people."

When Sekhmet Montu spoke of "our people," I turned to the northwest part of Liberation Square, where the monumental Egyptian Museum preserves many of the shrines, statues, sarcophagi, paintings, jewelry, grave goods, and mummies of the ancient Egyptians. I couldn't help asking her what she thought of the work of Egyptologists.

"When they work on the temples, that's fine with us," she stated. "But I become very angry when I think of them digging out our forefathers. To us, the spirit still needs the *khat* [body] to ascend into the otherworld, and what happens to it is of vital importance to the spirit. It's not really necessary to dig up bodies in order to find out how the people lived two or three thousand years ago. They've recently been digging in Giza in order to lay down a big water pipeline, and they've been discovering a great deal. Lucie Lamy [the stepdaughter of the hermetic philosopher R. A. Schwaller de Lubicz and the author of *Egyptian Mysteries*] learned a lot without digging up a lot of dead people. But naturally we can't speak out about this."

Heru was anxious to be off. He led his mother down a congested street as I trailed behind, trying to make sense of the unfathomable Cairene walking patterns. I barely managed to dodge undeviating, forward-moving bodies that edged me out into the street. It was a sweltering 105 degrees, but Sekhmet Montu and Heru were effortlessly making their way from one small shop to another, only to discover that Walkmans were out of stock everywhere. When I eventually caught up with them after each fruitless foray, Heru would give me a disappointed but philosophical look. Finally, in a little vendor's hut, we came across a man in a peach-colored caftan who presented us with a flimsy-looking red cassette machine into which he popped a tape of Egyptian popular songs. He placed some wobbly earphones over Heru's ears and watched the boy's eyes light up.

"You have to have a tape to go with the machine," I said to Heru.

His mother translated my remark, and after a short discussion Heru blurted out, "Elton John!"

Within minutes we came across all kinds of outdoor cassette racks stacked with innumerable Elton John tapes, each of them seeming to feature the song "Crocodile Rock." Heru chose one, and the tape went right into his machine, the earphones onto his head. Except for his shaved head and braided lock, he could have passed for a little American boy walking down some impassable city street, oblivious to the people and the noise.

Heru might have been oblivious, but as I fell behind him and his mother, I started to notice the staring that was taking place ahead of me. Almost every person, male or female, was unabashedly gawking at the little boy with his red Walkman, and at the woman with the nose ring and layered head scarves accompanying him. Not just staring, but snickering, pointing, making remarks, and laughing.

Sekhmet Montu turned around and saw me falling back because of the crowds and the heat, so she and Heru stopped for a minute until I caught up, then suggested we all go into a soda shop to drink some bottled water.

"It's amazing, all the hostile attention you get on the street," I told her.

"That's why my son and I go out as little as we can."

"Doesn't your husband worry about you?"

"Anywhere I am or where there's a large gathering of our people, the Shardana are there."

"The Shardana?"

"I can't say much about it except that it's the military aspect of our foundation, similar to the Ninja. You didn't see them, but every half-hour as we've been walking, someone has gone back to my husband and told him exactly where I am."

"Who's the head of the Shardana?"

"Generally, I am, though at the moment my husband's twin sister is acting head."

I found myself ordering two more bottles of water to quench my thirst as I considered the Ammonites' defense organization.

"But the Shardana can't protect you every minute," I remarked.

"But I have power of Hekau," she said to me. "The functions of Auset are my functions as well. Dark magic, which is *not* negative, is done in the hours of darkness through the powers of the moon. Light magic is done during the hours of the day with the powers of the sun. What people in the West understand as light [white] and dark [black] magic is in actuality positive and negative magic. It's magic that has been placed in the wrong time frame. Anything that's positive, if it's done at the wrong time, can be negative—and vice versa. It depends on the aim of the operator. I can do magic such that someone will move away from my area of influence. I can walk in the street and think a thought, and if I think it properly, with enough energy behind it, then if someone is trying to bother me, he'll turn around and walk away, shaking his head, wondering why he did that. I once knocked a man off his bicycle because he was intentionally coming at me and I didn't want to be run over by a bike! So defensive magic is what I use. To cause someone pain or kill a person is against the Forty-two Laws, unless it's in self-defense. Also, I can't do magic that will violate the free will of another person. I can, however, put an attractant for material things, as long as it doesn't violate anyone's free will."

It was still early afternoon when we returned to Sekhmet Montu's street. She asked me if I wished to come up to continue our conversation, and when I wondered if that was allowed when her husband was not present, she said that since her son was with her, it was permitted. Moreover, she informed me, it would make it impossible for her antagonistic neighbors to call her a whore, as one or two of them had previously done when someone had come to see her.

"Why do you stay in Cairo?" I asked her when we were in the sitting room, with Heru sitting next to me listening to Elton John.

"For the same reasons that Jews live in Israel, and Baha'is and Shiites live in Iran, and Kurds live in Iraq and Iran," she replied. "And because of our prophecies and because the gods were from this land, and our lives are directed to being close to the gods. If you can travel to the place of their birth, you're closer to them. This is holy land; our roots are here. And this is where we make our pilgrimages. We go to the places where the different parts of our Savior Ausar's body are supposed to have been buried—places like Abtu [Abydos] and the Temple of Horemheb; we go to the tomb of Tutankhamon, upraiser of the Faith of the Ancients and founder of the Ammonite Foundation; we go to the Tree of the Persea [now known as the Virgin's Tree, as legend has it that the Virgin and her child rested there during their flight into Egypt], where the God Ra, in its cat form, Mau, slew the serpent monster Apep; we go to Aswan—or Seyene, as it was called in ancient times—where two holy places were lost to us forever when the great dam was built, thus insulting Hapi [the God of the Nile in Inundation] and the cycle of God's creation. Our pilgrimages teach us that if we allow our laws to lapse or change, we will soon be as crumbled and lost as our ancient monuments.

"Since the days of the first Ammonite kingdoms outside Egypt, in Jordan, we've been wandering as freaks of the earth, but by being freaks we have kept the seed of truth alive. All I know is what I am here to fulfill, and that is our prophecies. It's prophesied that the Book will once again come into the hands of people because they'll want to understand it. It's not something that will be just a curiosity; they'll *believe* in it. And our people will once again live in the lands of Amman [Ammon] and Khem [Egypt]. But not by means of arms or theft: we'll be *asked* back. Egyptian culture will be resurrected. We cannot bring ourselves to life, however; someone else will resurrect us. And that's another reason why many people today are focusing on Auset: they're trying to resurrect Him through Her. The love, purity, self-sacrifice he represents *can* be resurrected.

"If you look at the story of Ausar, you'll notice that at first he wasn't actually dead, he was in a coma. What is a coma? It's a state of complete unawareness, and that's what the world has been in. People think they're awake and aware, but they aren't. To bring about the Hope [Heru], to make him manifest, people have to resurrect Ausar—they have to bring him out of the coma.

"Before Ausar and Auset lived, you died and then you lived again, you died and then you lived again. People were just recycling. There was no way to pass through the Hall of Judgment on into Paradise, into the Boat of Ra, which moves from this dimension to the next, giving continuity to the awareness of God. But because of both Ausar's and Auset's sacrifice for humanity, our souls and spirits and life essence were able to pass from this world into the more evolved states of creation."

"Whether or not Ausar and Auset are thought of as real or mythological," I said, "how do the Ammonites think of these two gods racially? Are they thought of as black or brown or white?"

"There are some books that say that Ausar was white and that he came into Egypt from Libya. Auset, on the other hand, came from the East, and she was yellow. This convergence was here in Africa, where the majority of the people are black. In the Nile Valley, during early times, there was every color of people. Some of us were white, some brown, some a kind of yellow color, some black. It depended on what part of the tribe you were from. And we have direct relation to the Dogon people in Mali. They tell the story that they went to the south and we went to the north, and that we will one day reunite. They call us the People of the Shining Faces and Those Who Write upon the Mountains with Fire. Also, there were a few Pharaohs who were black. There was no discrimination based on color here. We're all Nilotic people, and no race is exalted above another.

"But the Ammonites believe that you should marry within the faith and someone of your own genetic background and your own racial background: Rh-negative marries Rh-negative; Rh-positive, Rh-positive; brown marries brown; white, white; black, black. We see that God created every race for a purpose. There's a part of our writings that asserts that Auset created the brown people, Sekhmet Montu created the yellow people, Ra created the white people, and Heru created the black people. The writings also state that the blacks will be the salvation of humankind—the freeing of the black people will be the freeing of earth from the bonds of negativity and materialism—and that the Book will be given to all people when the black people are free. So if we can bring all of the colors of the earth into equality and bring forth the Hope, which *is* the black people, because Heru was black in his form of eternity, then the whole world will manifest the Holy Family."

"I gather that you have an elaborate set of teachings and laws," I mentioned to Sekhmet Montu.

"We've had these teachings for thousands of years, and there's a lot of symbolism in them that is meant to protect them from corrosion and corruption. Our version of the Isis tradition is pure because that's the way we kept it. But there are others, like the Shintoists in Japan, whose tradition of the Mother Goddess is pure too, because it belongs to them. We have a great respect for the American Indian tradition and regret that some of them have lost it because they converted to Christianity. We would rather have been wiped out than do that! We know of a secret group in Central America that puts up a figure of Mother Mary, and behind it is their own Mother Goddess; when they say the prayers to Mary, they're actually praying to the one behind.

"I've found that people in the West with their own Iseums or whatever don't want to have anything to do with us. They have their own little thing set up, they're happy with it, and they're not interested. They're mixing the Greeks and the Celtic and the Egyptian and the Hindu traditions all together, and you can't mix rays of energy like that and have it be safe. If you follow one line, follow that pattern. Stay with it. If you mix it up, *you* get mixed up, and you won't gain anything from it in the process. It *assures* reincarnation. Olivia Robertson and I have had a long correspondence about this, and she knows we disagree. I think it's terrific what she is doing, because there are a lot of people who would never have found Ausar and Auset except for her. It starts people searching, but it doesn't give people a system by which to arrive at a different point. The process of learning about the *neters* is a never-ending one. You can be a hundred and still discover things."

"What is your role in all this?" I asked.

"I have to mediate between the two tribes—the people who have the tradition and those who will be learning the tradition.

They have to be given the basic teachings, and then they themselves will grow a new shoot. These differences of manifestations
will make no difference to us, because theirs is a different society.

"The way I approach the teachings is not very traditional.
The teachers I had *were*, and still are, but I've taken the teachings
and applied them in a way that might prove more useful to others
today. And a lot of that, of course, has to do with my Western
education. You see, my family name, Amdid, literally means 'eater
of words.' Now, in my language, Pars-nawab, this is something
good, because it means that you take in knowledge. But to say
'Eat your words!' in English is something entirely different! So my
approach to the Book and the teachings attempts to bridge the
gap between the two worlds."

"How does one become an initiate?" I asked her.

"By first working through our thirty-six lessons."

Sekhmet Montu stood up, went into another room, and returned with a pile of folders.

"There are four levels," she said. "Level four consists of the
introductory lessons, Level three describes the *neters* and the principles, Level two explains the rituals and manifestations, and Level
one presents the Doctrine of the Faith, including the Twelve Laws
of Ammun-Ra and the Forty-two Laws of Aru. Then, after initiation, there's something else you study to become a priest, but I
can't tell you about that. I should say, however, that our people
don't make a decision to become Ammonites until they've reached
the age of reason. Once they've gone through the lessons, understood them, taken a vow to follow and to accept the codes we live
by, then they're considered members of the Ammonite community."

"These lessons are all in English," I commented after glancing
at them.

"The lessons, which are based on our oral tradition, were the collaboration of a number of Sau members and ourselves. But over the past two years they were put together, in the form you see them in now, mainly by four people: Sau Tahuti [the Ammonite high priest in the House of Mathematics and Astronomy], Senmut [Sekhmet Montu's personal scribe], His Excellency [her husband, Ptah Hotep], and myself. You'll see that the spelling and the English usage, which Senmut and I are responsible for, aren't always perfect, but we're working at it.

"As I've said, it's been prophesied that the Ammonites are to come out in this Age of Revelation; the doors will be open to the Western lands as well . . . and I have that much faith in God. In the past three years, for the first time, we have had students in countries like England, Germany, the United States, Nigeria, and Zaire studying this material and communicating with us about it. More than two hundred people have written to us, and right now there are five who are really sincere. A lot have delusions, a lot find the going too tough, a lot are belligerent, a lot find the teachings unacceptable. A few have difficulty receiving letters from us. Someone in a small town in Oklahoma asked us some questions, and we answered them—to us they were simple explanations— and we never heard from that person again. Or we get astonished letters saying, 'What have you done to me? What did you do that for?' And then there are the space cases. There was a guy who thought he was a manifestation of Ausar for ten days. He wrote a strange five-page letter to us that said, 'My girlfriend has left and she won't help me.' Isis told him goodbye, and he couldn't deal with it. He never realized that he wasn't Ausar and she wasn't Auset; otherwise she would never have walked out on him!

"I think that the teachings speak for themselves," Sekhmet Montu told me as she handed me the folders on my way out. "Take them with you, read them through, as much as you can, and maybe you can ask me about them when we see each other tomorrow."

Later, in my mercifully air-conditioned hotel room, I watched the sun drop across the Nile; and as an iridescent haze of red, pink, purple, and blood orange spread through the sky, I sat down at the desk and opened the folders that Sekhmet Montu had lent me. There I discovered an extensive and structured set of teachings that reminded me of the profound influence that the ancient Egyptian mysteries, from their beginnings, have had on many different schools of esoteric wisdom throughout the world.

Along with commentaries on subjects such as "The Concept of God," "Choosing and Finding a Way," and "Principles of Burial," the lessons included listings of Ammonite rituals—the Auset and Ausar Pageant, Day of the Persea Tree Blessing, Festival of the Opening of the Sky—and of the Twelve Opposites of Life: among them, Silence/Speaking, Insight/Narrow-mindedness, Truth/Falsity, Love/Cruel Love, Divinity/Holiness. There were detailed descriptions of Ammonite shrines and temples, diagrams of the Eternal Pyramid of Akhet-Ammun-Ra and of the Ogdoad ("the double faces of the four original faces of the God Force"), and numerous explanations of the major and minor *neters*. I found an assertion that just as the *neters* have male and female forms (Ammun/Ammunat, Ra/Raat, Neb Ptah/Nebt Sekhmet Montu), so a true Ammonite priesthood is a unit consisting of a priest and priestess, each of whom must be married to or have a lifetime contract with the other; a suggestion that all concepts, principles, ideas, laws, and rules in the Ammonite teachings—including, of course, the Twelve Laws of Ammun-Ra and the Forty-two Laws of Aru—should be applied in "three ways simultaneously: to the spirit, to the soul, to the body"; and a charming

Ammonite recipe for an Ausar wheat bread, meant to be used in a ceremony of blessing bread and consecrating wine:

Make an Ausar (Osiris) wheat bread. Place wheat seeds in a container, preferably square or oblong in this shape:

on 2 or 3 inches of soil. Then cover with 3 or 4 in. of soil, water it by sprayer and cover with a green (light) cloth on which are written or embroidered the words, "Hail Ausar, Lord of Bright Appearances, Thou art the resurrection, Thou art risen, O Un-nefer (The Beautiful One), Thou art risen and so am I, Thou germinateth and I germinate, Thou riseth triumphant and I rise triumphant through Thee. O Giver of the ressurected life, Thou art the sole Lord of evolution, Hail to Thee O Un-nefer! My Lord!"

Place in a warm place, but not in direct sunshine, until the sprouts appear out of the soil, taking care to spray/moisten the soil, but not overwater it.

When the sprouts are about 1½ to 2 in. tall, uncover the bed and expose the sprouts to the sunshine about 1 hour each day. The rest of the day place in indirect sunlight. The cloth should now be placed on the Altar where the bread is going to be placed when ready for the actual ceremony. When placing the cloth on the altar, say, "Even as I am placed in Paradise and Thou causest my place to be there ready, so now do ready Thy place, O Lord of Bright Appearances! Hail to Thee, O Un-nefer (The Beautiful One), Hail Ausar (Osiris)."

Now when the wheat seeds are tall enough, say 4–6 in. high, prepare the bread as usual (any recipe), but add a tblsp. of warm dark honey to the mixture when it is a paste. Knead and allow to rise; when risen, beat down and knead again, saying; "Thy enemies,

O Ausar, seek to confound Thy cycle, rise over them in the name of Thy Son, Neb Heru, who even now avenges Thee and in whose retinue, this, Thy humble servant is." Cover and allow to rise again. Before placing in the oven to bake, say, "Thy Majesty has risen, O Un-nefer, and I also and Thy bounty conquers hunger and feeds all, even the poor, and I shall eat of Thy seed and gain Eternal Life forever for Thou art risen Lord of Wonder."

Bake the bread in the shape of small round cakes, or if cake the same way.

When removing from the oven or fire say, "O Un-nefer, Thou hast recieved the warmth and love of Thy blessed wife, Auset (Isis) and the nourishment of the warmth of Thy Mother Nut and even now emerge victorious from Her Womb and give to those who partake of Thy seed vitality and life and warmth! The sweetness of Auset's love is within Thyself and it sweetens all who partake of Thy Faith. Rise up, O Bountiful One!"

Now you are ready for the ceremony.

Cover the "cakes" with a red cloth saying, "Thy sister/wife Auset, covers Thy form with Her Divine love and takes Thee to Thy place, which is even now awaiting You, to be adored by my-self, even as She adores Thee." Waving incence before the dish and walking backwards and repeating, "Hail Ammun-Ra, Lord of Light, Thy son Un-nefer is restored." Take the dish of bread into the temple or consecrated place and place it in the green cloth on the altar and cover it with this cloth saying, "Even as Auset pro-tects Thee, so does Thy rising protect Her also."

Then light incense and white candles saying, "O incense, food of the Divine, carry Thy sustenance to my Lord and Lady that They may know I am adoring Them both."

Then saying, "O Light of Ra, bringer of knowledge and true inner joy, grace the Risen Lord and the Lady of Motherhood with Thy rays of Light and Love." Saying, "O my Lord and Lady is cometh from my heart to You both, for You are what I love most!"

Now take the red wine and the white wine and place in two clear sided vessels; take from the red wine and add it to the white, saying, "Divinity is corrupted easily by evil from Holiness, May I never taint nor corrupt my Lady's heart by any action which I do."

Now take from the white wine and add it to another vessel of the red wine, saying, "Holiness is lost in Divinity and blessed by its union thereof and purified. Hail Mighty Lady Auset of Divineness who blessed Thy Brother three times! May I know Thy blessing of Divineness in all that I do."

Now sit, repeat whatever is in thy heart, wash thy heat with thy thoughts and be renewed. Then take of the bread and break it, saying, "O Auset, I am grateful for Thy gift of red grain and partake of Thy gift!" Eat then a piece. Drink then of the white wine, saying, "The Divinity of woman is upon my soul!" Then take another of the breads and break it, saying, "O Ausar, I am thankful for Thy gift of white grain and partake of Thy gift!" Eat then this bread. Drink of the red wine, saying, "The Holiness of man is upon my soul!"

Now take up the vessel which was white wine and which was tainted by the red, saying, "I cast out my abominations towards divinity and shall never act towards my mother Auset except in respect!" Cast out then this wine.

Now take up the vessel of red wine into which the white wine was added, saying, "My Holiness is blessed by the Divinity of the Mother and increased 10,000 fold. My Holiness is the resurrection of the Divinity of the Mother who lives in me. Together we are risen and live anew!" Drink then this wine.

You may leave the breads and wine for one hour as an offering to the *neters*, to partake of the essence of the same. Then take ⅔'s of it to those whom you love, or to other people, saying, "I am purified, I give bread to the hungry, wine to the thirsty, and my house is magnified by Ammun-Ra forever."

This may be done singly or in a group, taking care that each person partakes of the bread and wine in special vessels used in the ceremony. Then, when over, all may share in the remaining ⅓ after the hour is up.

When I visited Sekhmet Montu the next day, her husband rushed off to work upon my arrival, leaving Heru to act as the requisite chaperon. Then she told me a little bit about her previous incarnations.

"I've always been in the service of the gods in one way or another, even in other lifetimes," she stated. "I'm not a new spirit on this plane; I've been here a long time, and I still have the things I learned in past lives within me, and they're a natural part of me. When I first came back to Cairo with my husband, we were up in Ali Pasha Square, near the Sayyiana el-Husein Mosque. We took a walk up there—it was late in the evening, midnight or one A.M.—and all of a sudden I had a vision that hit me in the face, in which I and my husband were run down by a chariot and killed right on that spot. But why should I try to relive these kinds of traumas? Maybe it was a kind of warning: to wake up, pay attention in the *present*.

"People say, 'I'm this incarnation,' 'I'm that incarnation.' What I'd say to them is, if you *are* that incarnation, why are you still here? What kind of mistakes did you make in that incarnation? Take your ego out of it and try to learn from what you did then so that you can repair things now and not have to return.

"When I finally did come back into this lifetime, spiritually I was almost dead; and if it hadn't been for the help of my husband, whose *neter* is Anpu, a guide not only in the afterworld but here in this world as well, and for Sau Tahuti, who put a protection on me, and for a few others, my energy would have completely failed me."

"You've mentioned Sau Tahuti to me before," I interjected. "Who is he?"

"He's the high priest of the House of Tahuti [Thoth], and he sits on the Sau Council. He's more than one hundred years old, and he's not reincarnated. He has figured out some system, beyond my comprehension, whereby he can pass from one body, the old body, into another body directly in this world. He's been doing this for a couple of thousand years. And he carries all of his wisdom, including astrology and mathematics, of whose House he is high priest, with him when he changes. He knows when his body is going to die, and he's got another one already prepared."

I was looking at Sekhmet Montu quizzically, so she said, "I see that you don't understand. If you read the novel *The Egyptian* [by the Finnish writer Mika Waltari, published in 1945], you'll find a description of an old man who can cast his essence into another body that he has made. *That's* Sau Tahuti! He has a wife and a baby, and that baby has no soul and no spirit. When Sau Tahuti's body dies, *his* soul and spirit move into that baby's body. . . . You see, not everybody has a soul, and not everybody has a spirit. The majority of the people you observe walking around are just bodies; they have life essence only."

As was her wont, Sekhmet Montu related this to me in a resolute but plain and unemphatic tone of voice. Heru, meanwhile, had retired to his room, where he was making three-dimensional figures of cars out of paper and listening over and over to a scratchy record of American and English children's songs, all sung in exactly the same chirpy, robotic manner, on his portable record player. So for the next hour I listened to Sekhmet Montu describe her Ausetian self against the background accompaniment of "Ring Around the Rosie," "Old MacDonald Had a Farm," "A Bicycle Built for Two," "My Darling Clementine," "The Sidewalks of New York," "Humpty Dumpty," and "We Wish You a Merry Christmas."

Sekhmet Montu picked up a writing pad she had been holding in her lap.

"I jotted down some notes last night," she said, "to help me explain that in my manifestation of Auset, the body of Ausar was, for me, *the world we live in.* Now, what do I mean by that? There are seven continents in the world, divided into two parts, the north and the south, which adds up to fourteen—the fourteen pieces of Ausar's dismembered body. There are also the North and the South Pole, which represent the two nonphysical parts of Ausar, his soul and his spirit, from which the confusion of fourteen and sixteen parts comes about today.

"At one time, all these continents were one huge landmass that split up. So the story of Auset and Ausar can be translated into the story of the physical world itself. I spent a lifetime in each of the continents—two lifetimes in each continent, north and south—and this was a spiritual representation of the gathering together of the fourteen parts of Ausar's body. In another sense, since the body of Ausar also represents the faith, which was dismembered as well, by going through those physical lifetimes I was able to understand different things from each of these places, and this had to do with bringing the faith back together.

"So I've managed to bring all these pieces together within myself, just as Auset did. But on another level, I had to suffer the dismemberment of *my* life, through many lifetimes of learning, in order to be able to manifest him as well. The heart of Ausar was dismembered because her heart was him, and his heart was her! This is why the story of Ausar and Auset is such a great love story—they were inseparable. You cannot separate one heart even if it's in two bodies. By bringing him together, she brought her own heart to a point where she could heal it.

"But I couldn't make this sacrifice alone. My husband has also made this sacrifice, because we are spiritually one. He has followed me through all of my lifetimes, and when I've been in difficulty, he has been there to help me out. We haven't necessarily always been together or married. But he has always been there to guide me. The sacrifice is complete, and it's now possible for us to be reunited. It is complete contentment. We never argue, since our soul and our spirit are in complete harmony. How could we live any other way and manifest what we believe? It wouldn't be possible."

When I returned the following day, a Friday, the sounds of muezzins and Koranic tapes all over the neighborhood reminded me that it was the Muslim sabbath. Up in their apartment, Sekhmet Montu, Ptah Hotep, and Neb Heru were awaiting me, splendidly attired in ceremonial garb, which they were wearing both to worship in their family shrine and to show me how they dressed to perform their priestly functions.

Sekhmet Montu wore a yellow blouse and an ankle-length red skirt. On the front of the skirt were displayed the hieroglyphs for the Goddess Sekhmet and the phrase *Ab-khu-à,* meaning "I am pure." On the left shoulder of the blouse were depicted olive branches, representing physical peace; a small oil lamp, signifying the light within; the Crown of the North and the Crown of the South; and the Book, with a crook, a flail, and the staff of power behind it. On the back were two solar barks, the emblem of the Great House. Her extraordinary necklace consisted of a gold-and-turquoise disk, representing the temples with the steps of initiation; the symbol of Ra with the arrows of Neith, Goddess of War; and twelve bells, each indicating one of the gods of creation. On her ears hung pendants of Auset, and on her right hand was a striking ring, a scarab with a serpent and the scepter of power on either side, signifying her reign.

Ptah Hotep was dressed in a white robe; imitation leopard-skin made of cotton, representing the priesthood; and the dark green cummerbund of Ausar with the sign of Ra on it. Neb Heru was wearing a long Pakistani-type shirt, dark trousers gathered at the bottom and buttoned on the outside, a dark green cummerbund designating him as the son of Ausar, and basketball sneakers (signifying, perhaps, that he was nine years old). He also carried a little sword that he had made himself. "He thinks it's like the sword that Heru the Avenger carried," said his mother.

Heru approached me and presented me with a statuette of Horus of the Double Horizon embodied as a golden falcon. I thanked him for his generosity but was a bit reluctant to accept a second *neter* figurine from the family. Noticing my hesitancy, however, Sekhmet Montu told me firmly, "If the god comes to you, you cannot refuse it!"

Ptah Hotep now made a deep bow to Sekhmet Montu, bent down to kiss her feet, and placed some oil of myrrh on her forehead ("He was honoring my manifestation of divinity," she explained later, "not *me*"). He next offered some frankincense to the principle of holiness, then proceeded to burn a mixture of incense on dried orange peels, using a flail to spread the scented smoke around the apartment. "We have to do this in order to purify everything," Sekhmet Montu told me, referring to the omnipresent calls to prayer coming in through the window. "It's something defensive we do to separate our energies from the Muslims'. If we didn't do this, we'd be overwhelmed by the energy they put out."

Ptah Hotep took out a set of keys and opened a padlock on the door at the far end of the sitting room. What was inside was amazing to behold: on a large white-cloth–covered table, taking up three quarters of the small room, were a series of painted statuettes, like those I had been given, of the major Egyptian *neters*. Heru and Het Heru, Nebt Het and Khonsu, Nebt Sekhmet Montu and Neb Ptah, and Ausar and Auset were standing together, the members of each couple at the right and left sides of the table. In the center were the figures of Tahuti and Ma'at, the Bull of Ammun, and a model of the Ark of Ra and of the Sanctuary, in which, I was told, Ammun/Ammunat was hidden behind closed doors. The replica of another door, resting in the middle of the table, represented the Way to Paradise. In the midst of all of this were offering bowls and urns, candles and flowers, ankhs and unguent jars.

When we approached the table, Sekhmet Montu showed me a twisted stick from the sacred Persea Tree in Heliopolis; burial instruments and other instruments made from magnetized metals found near the Citadel in Cairo; and holy water, in little jars, from Abdu, Heliopolis, and the Nile.

Ptah Hotep entered the room, prostrated himself, offered incense, lit some candles, then recited a beautiful noonday prayer, which Sekhmet Montu repeated in English just after him.

> O Ammun-Ra, Light of Lights, Sun of all Suns, at the zenith of your power that breathes life to all and redeems through death, that the never-ending cycle may be forever, my power is with You; for I am You. Beautiful are all the things You have created; Wondrous is all the Universe; Glorious are all the things that You have made. O light Ammun-Ra Eternal, I am still with You. Praise to You, Ammun-Ra, forever.

"Am I allowed to sit in the shrine room by myself?" I asked Sekhmet Montu.

"Of course," she said as they both walked out and shut the door.

I sat on the floor on a small mat and rested against a wall. The Egyptian sun was blazing through a window into the room. In this realm of the gods, it seemed as if the numerous painted red and green and blue and black and white statuettes had a life of their own, like creatures in a fairy tale who become themselves when all doors are closed and who can be seen only by those who believe. I imagined being in the Outer Temple of this shrine, looking through a glass darkly into the heart of the Inner Temple, with its Ark of Ra and the Holy of Holies—a world of Hidden Light.

When I emerged from the shrine, I heard knocking at the front door. Ptah Hotep quickly padlocked the shrine room and went to see who was in the hallway.

"As you can imagine," Sekhmet Montu told me, "the shrine room is always locked, since we just can't take any chances."

We all listened as Ptah Hotep said something in Arabic to a person outside, then closed the door and returned to assure his wife that everything was fine.

As I sat down on the couch, Heru, now with his Walkman, came and sat down right next to me.

"What about him?" I asked Sekhmet Montu, gesturing toward the sweet, wise little boy on my right.

"We bring our son up as a *child*—a gifted child, and a very loved one. We want to educate him as much as possible, but we leave it to him to bring the god out, because it's his choice whether he manifests or not. We know it's in there—that's enough for us. I answer his questions as best as I can. But I don't push him to be what I know he is; I don't brainwash him.

"He asked me if he could learn the Medu when he was five. And one night just last week, he came and said to me that when his father and I died, he was going to bury us and mummify us as best as he could—he helped us mummify our dog when it died—and close us in a glass case and put us away where no one could find us, and he'd place the Book in our hands so that we'd have it when we went through the Hall of Judgment. And then he was going to cry around this glass box, and everywhere he cried, a lotus or a rose was going to grow. I'd never told him that the tears of Heru bring forth flowers; he hasn't reached that point in his studies. Now, how would a normal child be able to come up with something like that?

"In one of the old stories it's told that when Setekh was fighting Heru, he gained control over him with his semen, and then

Heru did the same thing to Setekh. When our son was five years old, he found a picture of Setekh somewhere, and he tore it up into little pieces, put it in a plastic bag, and peed all over it. And then he took it and flushed it down the toilet. And I'd never told him that story! He wanted to set it on fire, but I thought he was a little young!

"Last year I was doing some magic here to open a new circle, and I was burning incense all through the house because we were having some difficulty with people—a lot of negativity. And without being told, he started pulling out hairs from his sidelock and putting them in the fire. He told me they were serpents, and that when the serpents died we wouldn't have any more problems. Again, he'd never been with me when I made wax serpents inside a magic circle, hacked them into pieces, stomped on them, and said the appropriate *hekau* over it. And two days after Neb Heru pulled out his hair, the troubles went away."

"So your son's role is destined?" I asked.

"It's in the prophecies that when this new era was to begin, he would incarnate again—the Heru god-being incarnate—to avenge his father and to give new life to the hope that has always been in the world . . . and that he will lead people who are in the darkness *out* of the darkness.

"My son can accept or reject his role. I'm the active Per-āa right now because he hasn't made his decision yet. And what will determine what he decides will be humankind itself—whether it continues on the path of destruction or begins to turn around. He is here. He kept the promise he made that he would return when he was needed. If people avail themselves of the power that is within him, that's up to them."

"How do the Ammonites think of him?" I wondered.

"As far as being accepted by the Ammonites, I don't think there is a family in the whole community anywhere in the world that didn't kill a sheep the day he was born. He knows that people believe this about him, but I don't think that he has decided to bring it out on his own. There have been times I've seen it shine through, as I've recounted to you, but it's not something he tries to deal with every day. He has to be taught and disciplined, just like anyone else. If he went out and told everyone on the street what we believe without using the Twelve Opposites of Life, he could get us all wiped out! Even God has to follow the laws of the universe.

"We don't say that we're the only religion—we aren't. There are all kinds of different pagan religions. And we all have different things to offer and different means of spiritual development and evolution. *They're* not wrong and *we're* not wrong; we're just at different points of awareness. But I want people to understand that we *are* here—we've always been here. And they have to be open to accepting that before Heru can manifest. If they're full of scepticism, there's no way he'll step forth."

During my stay in Cairo, I tried many times, and in many different ways, to find out definitively where Sekhmet Montu was really from. Her American English was so fluent, so idiomatic, that it was difficult to believe that she hadn't had at least one full incarnation somewhere in the southwestern United States—though *only* one, since she did, after all, speak fluent Pars-nawab, a bit of Arabic, and all the Medu she needed for her ceremonial duties.

At one point in our conversations, she brought out and showed me three "world birth certificates" from the World Service Authority in Beirut, an organization that promotes world citizenship and issues passports, identity cards, and birth certificates. One of these gave her name as Sekhmet Montu Amdid and listed her occupation as housewife. Her husband's certificate listed him as Ptah-Besa Amdid and his occupation as "priest/educator/Doctor of Divinity/B.A. Management." "He's a nondenominational priest recognized in the West," Sekhmet Montu said. Her son was identified as Heru-Kuti-Ptah Amdid, and his eyes were described as blue.

Sekhmet Montu put the certificates back in an envelope and said to me, "All this may be true or not true. Remember, we don't have any papers when we come into the world. I could buy a paper to say where I was born. People in the Middle East can acquire necessary identification papers and birth certificates because of the turmoil that always exists here. People have learned many ways to survive that are unnecessary in the West. It's not easy, but if I needed to do so, I would buy another paper to contradict the first one, and no one would know which was true!

"What name I use is not important. I know my spiritual name; my people recognize me for what I am. You can't tell Auset to lift her veil and reveal her face. She won't do it. You have to earn the right to see it. If these people want to know how I got to be what I am, they have to try to be *as* I am . . . and they will understand *exactly* how I got here. And the material manifestation of how I got here will then be irrelevant."

When I was taking leave of this Ammonite family for the last time, Sekhmet Montu presented me with a statuette of the crowned Auset, painted blue and gold and red. Heru held my hand, and Ptah Hotep bowed and spoke some words in Parsnawab, which his wife translated: "He hopes that Anpu will travel with you, that by the will of Ausar there will be no difficulty between us, and that anytime you come to Egypt you're welcome in our house. Without invitation. Just knock on the door."

I thanked him, and we all said goodbye. Ptah Hotep's final

words to me were "When you see Ausar in the otherworld, that will be enough."

The night before I flew back to the United States, I placed the statuettes of Auset, Ausar, and Heru on top of one of my suitcases to make sure I wouldn't forget them. When I opened my eyes the next morning and saw them standing there together, hawk-headed son in between his two crowned parents, it was as if I had dreamed a dream in which Isis, Osiris, and Horus had come to life in the city of Cairo where I had walked through sweltering, crowded streets and bought a little red Walkman for the child who might—(who knows?)—one day be the Hope of the World.

From the Ammonite Calendar for the year 12,453 (1992). Drawn by
H. G. Sekhmet Montu.

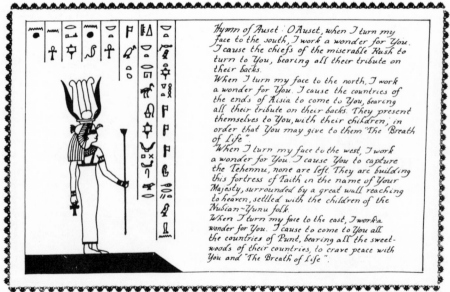

Hymn of Ausar : Hail to You, King of Kings! Lord of
lords! Prince of Princes! Possessor of the two lands,
even from the womb of Your Mother, Nut. Ruler of
all the Lands of Agert! Gold are Your limbs,
lapis-lazuli Your Head, turquoise Your Hands,
Pillar of Millions! Beautiful of Face in the
Sacred Lands! Grant me splendour in heaven,
power on earth, and an aquital in Neterkhert,
and a sailing downstream as a Soul-Living
to Per-ba-let and a sailing upstream to
Abtu as a Bennu, and a going in and a
coming out!

Hymn of Auset : O Auset, when I turn my
face to the south, I work a wonder for You.
I cause the chiefs of the miserable Kush to
turn to You, bearing all their tribute on
their backs.
When I turn my face to the north, I work
a wonder for You. I cause the countries of
the ends of Aisia to come to You, bearing
all their tribute on their backs. They present
themselves to You, with their children, in
order that You may give to them "The Breath
of Life".
When I turn my face to the west, I work
a wonder for You. I cause You to capture
the Tehennu, none are left. They are building
this fortress of Taith in the name of Your
Majesty, surrounded by a great wall reaching
to heaven, settled with the children of the
Nubian-Yunu folk.
When I turn my face to the east, I work a
wonder for You. I cause to come to You all
the countries of Punt, bearing all the sweet-
woods of their countries, to crave peace with
You and "The Breath of Life".

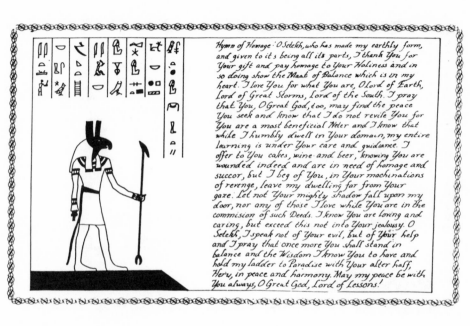

Hymn of Homage: O Setekh, who has made my earthly form, and given to it's being all its parts, I thank You for Your gift and pay homage to Your Holiness and in so doing show the Maat of Balance which is in my heart. I love You for what You are, O Lord of Earth, Lord of Great Storms, Lord of the South. I pray that You, O Great God, too, may find the peace You seek and know that I do not revile You for You are a most beneficial Neter and I know that while I humbly dwell in Your domain, my entire learning is under Your care and guidance. I offer to You cakes, wine and beer, knowing You are wounded indeed and are in need of homage and succor, but I beg of You, in Your machinations of revenge, leave my dwelling far from Your gaze. Let not Your mighty shadow fall upon my door, nor any of those I love while You are in the commission of such Deeds. I know You are loving and caring, but exceed this not into Your jealousy. O Setekh, I speak not of Your evil, but of Your help and I pray that once more You shall stand in balance and the Wisdom I know You to have and hold my ladder to Paradise with Your alter half, Heru, in peace and harmony. May my peace be with You always, O Great God, Lord of Lessons!

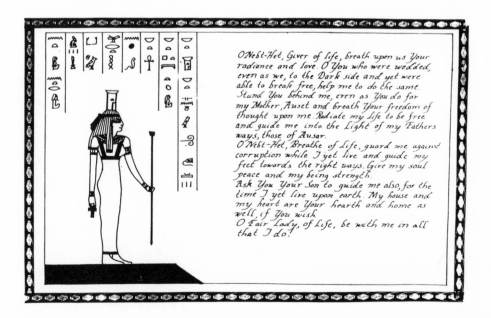

O Nebt-Het, Giver of life, breath upon us Your radiance and love. O You who were wedded, even as we, to the Dark side and yet were able to break free, help me to do the same. Stand You behind me, even as You do for my Mother, Auset and breath Your freedom of thought upon me. Radiate my life to be free and guide me into the Light of my Fathers ways, those of Ausar.
O Nebt-Het, Breathe of Life, guard me against corruption while I yet live and guide my feet towards the right ways. Give my soul peace and my being strength.
Ask You Your Son to guide me also, for the time I yet live upon earth. My house and my heart are Your hearth and home as well, if You wish.
O Fair Lady, of Life, be with me in all that I do!

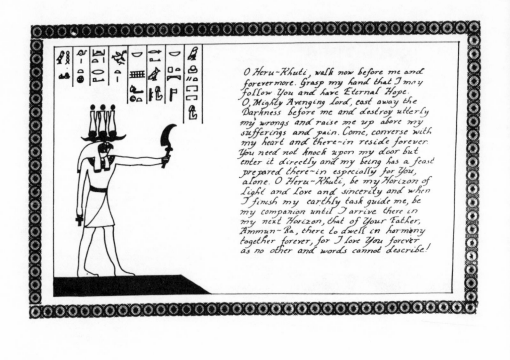

O Heru-Khuti, walk now before me and forevermore. Grasp my hand that I may follow You and have Eternal Hope. O, Mighty Avenging Lord, cast away the Darkness before me and destroy utterly my wrongs and raise me up above my sufferings and pain. Come, converse with my heart and there-in reside forever. You need not knock upon my door but enter it directly and my being has a feast prepared there-in especially for You, alone. O Heru-Khuti, be my Horizon of Light and Love and sincerity and when I finish my earthly task guide me, be my companion until I arrive there in my next Horizon, that of Your Father, Ammun-Ra, there to dwell in harmony together forever, for I love You forever as no other and words cannot describe!

ISIS AND OSIRIS:

A Conversation with

Mark Hasselriis

Mark Hasselriis, an artist and lecturer, served as artist and draftsman for the epigraphic survey at Khonsu and Medinet Habu temples for the Oriental Institute of the University of Chicago. As an artist in the Bollingen Foundation expedition, he helped record the great tomb of Rameses VI and the shrines of Tutankhamon. In the late 1980s, I attended a number of Hasselriis' lectures on the symbolism of ancient Egyptian religion at the School of Sacred Arts in New York City. In these revelatory talks, Hasselriis worked with images from papyri and wall reliefs and drew on number symbolism, zodiacal associations, the kundalini tradition, esoteric wisdom, Jungian psychology, and mainstream Egyptology as a way of entering into the ancient Egyptian way of seeing and knowing.

Hasselriis credits his unusual approach to sacred painting and mythology to Natasha Rambova (1897–1966), the second wife of Rudolph Valentino—artist, costume designer, and research fellow at the Bollingen Foundation—with whom in the 1950s he studied the basic patterns of Egyptian, Babylonian, and Greek symbolism. Some of Rambova's other students at that time included the anthropologist Maud Oakes, the professor of Indian art Stella Kramrisch, the artist and writer Mai Mai Sze, and the photographer, writer, and editor Dorothy Norman, for whose book *The Hero: Myth/Image/Symbol* (1969) Hasselriis supplied line drawings. It was in the garden of Dorothy Norman's Easthampton vacation home that I spent an August afternoon in 1992. There, among flowering gardenias, geraniums, hibiscus, and roses, and under a very hot sun, Mark Hasselriis explained and illuminated for me the connections between Egyptian mythology and the doctrine of chakras in the Indian kundalini system of yoga:

We could say that chakras are centers in the psychophysical structure of man that accord with the seven constituents of man, along with the link that draws them together, namely the human backbone. (See Illustration 7.1.) So the first chakra

7.1: *Seven lotus centers of the kundalini.*

corresponds to the physical body; the second represents the lower soul; the third is the seat of the instinctive mind; the fourth is the heart center, of desire-mind; the fifth is the higher mind, or *manas*; the sixth is the center of higher soul, or *bodhi*, which is associated with the command center and the third eye, and which is also divine intuition; and the seventh is the seat of the spirit, the consciousness principle, which the Theosophists call the sheath of the monad and what Jung calls the self. The self also embodies all of the others within a totality.

Now, what connects the seven chakras to ancient Egyptian cosmology and to the ancient Egyptian gods? Let's start off with the cosmology. The seven centers of kundalini represent the seven metaphorical rungs of the ladder, what Joseph Campbell calls the "lotus ladder," leading from matter to spirit. In the Egyptian view, man is a microcosm of the cosmic pattern; he carries it within him. In India, too, the kundalini represents a microcosm of the universal cosmology. Brahma dwells at the seventh chakra; the earth is the first chakra. Stella Kramrisch points out that the Hindu temple has a hole at the top, representing egress to the transcendent realm of the *parusha*, the heavenly man, which or whom the temple personifies in stone. And it's the same in Egypt, where the Holy of Holies represents the heights.

Take the pyramid. The pyramid is the stairway to heaven—again, a ladder image. It's also the mountain of the god, in which the dead god is buried, like a seed in the earth, his soul flying up to the heights through little open passageways. And at the height of the pyramid is Atum, the supreme principle. So the stairway is the image of the depths connected to the heights, the objective world connected to the spiritual world.

Now, the four lower rungs of kundalini deal with the physical, the emotional, the instinctive, and the human mental levels, corresponding to the four elements and the four kingdoms—mineral, vegetable, animal, man. The ancients may not have been scientifically informed, but they weren't stupid. And they knew that snakes and crocodiles belonged to an order prior to the creation of mammals. The Egyptians certainly knew this, and although they didn't have a concept of physical science in the usual sense of the word, there *is* a tradition that sheds light on their thinking.

Certain Gnostic schools held that there are three kinds of people: first, the *hylic*, whose only interest or focus in life is pure physicality and instinctive response; second, the *psychic*, who are striving to attain something, to rise higher, who are on the path of individuation, and who have a chance of passing the Judgment, which in Greek was called the psychostasis; and third, the *pneumatic*, whose perspective is a philosophical peace and who have evolved to a spiritual level such that their place in the afterlife is assured.

So look at what this says. Those who don't pass beyond the nose of Ammut [the hippo/crocodile/lioness demon who devours the souls of the condemned; see Illustration 7.2], who fall back and dissolve and return to the source, these are the *hylic* people. Those whose hearts are in the balance, being weighed, are frequently engaged in inner struggle to find themselves and their values. These are the *psychic* people, and the weighing of the heart, or the soul, relates to them. A pair of golden scales were found in Crete, and engraved on each pan of the scales was a butterfly, which is the Greek or pre-Greek image of psyche, the soul. There's a different perspective in the Greek tradition, but it's only slight, because in the Egyptian view the heart (chakra four) is tied to the soul—the lower soul (chakra two) and also the higher soul (chakra six). Or, one might say, the Heart of Osiris (chakra four) lies in between the goddesses Nephthys (chakra two) and Isis (chakra six).

A number of years ago, a student of mine brought to my attention the Nineteenth Dynasty Leiden Papyrus, which depicts the Judgment Hall scene I was just referring to. He said to me, "Do you think this has anything to do with kundalini?" Among other things, I noticed the three "chakras," or dots, under the nose of the frightening tripartite animal. I noticed that the foot of the baboon, Thoth, was on the level of the fourth chakra. I noticed that the Goddess Isis was touching the sixth chakra. I knew that Aphrodite and the Great Mother

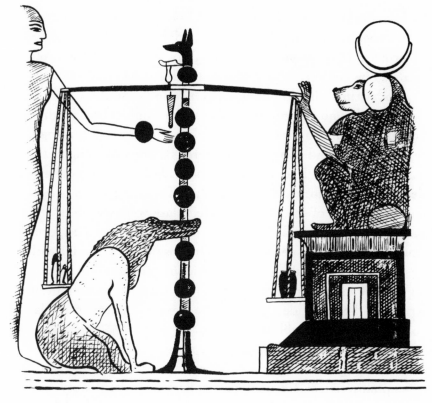

7.2.

goddesses were associated with that number. And when I showed a slide of this vignette at the lecture, my student jumped up and exclaimed, "They had it, they had it!"

You see, the importance of finding kundalini in Egypt at this date, around 1300 B.C., is that it is the earliest picture of the tradition to exist *anywhere*. No Indian example exists that is more than, at best, a century or so old. Some very early Indian art may hint at it, but we don't know for certain. Also, it is an esoteric tradition as far as practice is concerned, and it is initiatory. It is not for the dead but for *living* candidates to wisdom, and it supports the idea that a living individual may pass through the judgment process *before* death. Such is the mystery "death" of initiates.

Kundalini is not a posthumous yoga. There is no evidence,

to be sure, that the Egyptians practiced *asanas* or postures of hatha yoga or the like. However, kundalini *sakti* [energy] can be aroused or awakened also through purely mental yoga, and can also be conferred by a knowledgeable teacher.

Today, in India, kundalini yoga is known by thousands of people, although it is probable that at most only a few hundred actually attempt to practice it as a discipline, and of these still fewer succeed and experience full arousal or awakening of the "serpent power." It is similarly likely, despite the scant evidence available to us, that only a handful of Egyptian priests and priestesses of the most educated class were aware of this particular esoteric tradition and its psychophysical aspects. The philosophical aspect—that is, the cosmological ladder with its seven steps—could have been known generally not only in Egypt but in Mesopotamia, where the ziggurat reflects in its structure the same idea, as does the Egyptian pyramid or Jacob's ladder in the biblical tradition.

Only certain temperaments are actually suited to practice kundalini yoga, but anyone may derive benefit from the study of its philosophical, spiritual, psychological, or "septenary" implications, some of which were rediscovered in Italy during the Renaissance and appear in art from Siena. In any case, I want to make it clear that Egyptian religion encompassed far more than is reflected in kundalini, even though the ladder or the steps-to-heaven-from-the-netherworld appears as an image during the pyramid age and sets one to thinking and asking, "How early *did* this tradition first appear, and where did it originally come from?"

But can one go from this and suggest that the Egyptian gods are *embodiments* of chakras? I think it's subtler than that. I can say that Nephthys represents the second chakra and her sister Isis the sixth, because that's their sphere of operation. The chakras, more accurately put, embody divine powers, rather than the reverse. On one level Osiris represents the spirit, on another the heart—number seven and number four . . . and he's even number one because he's a dead body! The heights and depths are the same. That's the point! You live by passing, first from number seven, the source, into manifestation. Because everything that happens is a result of the passage of time. Manifestation means that we live through childhood, youth, maturity, old age—time brings the unfolding.

Osiris' brother Set is associated with the third chakra, but he influences all the others, just as your solar plexus may influence your heart or any other part of you. Here, number three has to do with the instinctive realm. And Set is the natural opposition to Horus. Because Horus and Set are really dual figures. There is in fact a drawing showing Horus and Set joined in one double-headed body, with the bows on which the serpents stand representing Upper and Lower Egypt, combined in one individual, while the serpents represent creative energy (see Illustration 7.3). The word "Horus," according to Professor Robert Bianchi, means "lofty." He is the lofty spirit of aspiration. Set is what drags it down, or tries to oppose it.

7.3: His two faces in the mysteries. Tomb of Rameses VI, Thebes.
C. 1200–1085 B.C.

Set is the *unevolved* desire, Horus the *evolving* desire. However, evil is not explained in a few words, naturally.

It's all very well to say that God is good, that the angels are sweet, that we should be moral and ethical—to say that is to *recognize* number five. If you don't *do* anything about it, however, you're still dominated by chakra three. And three has the power: Set is the animal vitality that has to be controlled—anger, hatred, rebelliousness. It's the third chakra where Set and Horus battle—right in the solar plexus. *And* in the heart. When you get above the heart, you're entering into the divine world. The heart is where the transformation takes place. You leave the four elements and begin to move into ether and the higher spiritual elements, which are abstract and formless. So the four is also a battleground.

One might see the encounter between Set and Horus as a kind of kundalini warfare. It's the battle of the unevolved energies against the forces that are learning and controlling. Horus *learns* how to control; he is a learning god, which is why he's a child on earth or in time. He has to grow from childhood to become the embodiment of all the divine powers in order to achieve order. So at one moment he's shown with a sidelock, sitting in the lap of Isis, his mother. That's his early stage of initiation. Later on, though, when he has to learn other lessons, he's shown sitting on the lap of Sekhmet, the lion-headed goddess. That's the initiation the king goes through to learn about power, which is a hard lesson: trust no one, take responsibility, use your strength wisely. And these are two aspects of the same goddess.

Now, on that "lotus ladder," you climb from the bottom up—and then there is the struggle to awaken in the midpoint of the netherworld, which corresponds to the bottom. Horus comes to life at the midpoint, in the pit of the underworld. That's the awakening of the Horian principle, of the principle of aspiration. That is probably why, when the Buddha was asked whether or not there was anything that was genuinely a miracle, he is said to have replied, "The change of heart is a genuine miracle" (though the text I read used the Greek word *metanoia*, which means "change of mind"). This change of mind/heart that leads to spiritual awakening takes place as part of the process of judgment before Osiris. Without that awakening, there can be no self-evaluation of one's moral life. It's one thing to say, as I heard a lecturer once do, that the judgment is meant to determine a person's "social acceptability." That is, you pass before the Judgment of Osiris to determine whether you're fit to live with the others in the hereafter. As in a country club! And I listened to that lecturer and said to myself, "Yes, that's true, but that's only half the equation"; and the other half is the most important one. If the awakening doesn't occur within the person, then that person perhaps falls back into the purely instinctual realm, under the nose of Ammut—the lower three chakras, the animal world. There are also greater and lesser degrees of awakening.

Now, I haven't said anything about Isis' sister Nephthys, who is the *ka*, or vital energy, of the gods and who represents the instinctive realm of feeling and emotion. When you feel good, you're up; when you feel down, you're crushed. Your physical vitality changes because of your emotional vitality. Nephthys is very emotional. Isis is cool-headed; Isis knows what she's doing; Nephthys can have a temper tantrum.

The name Nephthys means "lady of the house." *Your* emotional nature, *my* emotional nature, is the lady in our house. Say the wrong thing and she gets all excited. She's an aspect of the psyche that's in women and men. When Jung, talking about the psyche, refers to the woman who opposes or lures the man, that's either Nephthys or Isis. And they merge and unmerge. When she's wise and leading you on toward wisdom or integration, then she's Isis, but when she's emotional or hysterical or tempting you like Aphrodite, then she's Nephthys.

Together, Nephthys and Isis represent wisdom and emotional wholeness—things working in the right way, the way they're *supposed* to work. People will cynically say that they don't. But when things evolve and are elevated to a higher state, they largely *do* work in that way, as in times of peace or during cultural golden ages. But first it must occur within the individual.

Isis is often shown receiving the Boat of the Sun at sunset, and Nephthys receiving it in the morning at the eastern horizon. I used to think it should be the other way around, since Nephthys isn't the "wise" one. But the answer is that Isis is experience and knowledge and the mother, full of love, who takes the sun into the west; Nephthys is the vitality that *enables* the sun to rise in the east. You enter into new life with Nephthys energizing you—that's the divine child.

Nephthys is like a wet nurse. Remember, Isis is alone in the northern bulrushes because she has to give birth to her child by means of a higher power. But her sister Nephthys loves and assists her, and even hides her—she tries to fool her husband Set into looking the other way. But Anubis first gathers the pieces of Osiris' body together and embalms them. Neither he nor, certainly, Nephthys can add the magical power of life itself. It's Isis who integrates Osiris and conceives Horus by him, and then Horus subsequently supports his father spiritually.

As for Anubis, he is the desire, in the everyday sense, the *personal* desire that leads through life, though we pay but scant attention to it. And of course he leads the dead person through death, embalms him, and guides him to the Judgment Hall in the middle of the netherworld. And why a jackal? A jackal is a pathfinder. He knows where water is in the desert, and like a dog he is faithful.

What does it mean that Anubis is the offspring of Osiris and Nephthys? Horus, we know, is the son of Osiris and Isis. Horus is the way in which death will be overcome, evil will be undone, and order will be established. And wisdom has to be the mother of that. That's Isis. She's the one who gives birth to the fighter, the mind that has aspiration.

But there's another side to life. We're led through experiences in order to learn about physical and sexual things, to learn how to live in our bodies—that's our *pre*education, that's before we get a spiritual education. And that takes place down in our emotions. A young person goes out with adventure in his or her heart. And Anubis is the adventure in the heart.

I had a dream when I was fifteen that I was led into a funeral by a little dog with a rose tied to its neck. And the dog was black and white. In other words, the experience I was encountering was both good and bad. It was a white dog with black spots, with a rose tied to its collar. The rose was love. Love was leading me into the realm of experience, of disillusionment, of death. But I wouldn't have grown up as a human being if I hadn't ventured into risky quarters. Love is desire.

In Finistère in Brittany, it's believed that dogs lead people at death to the Blessed Isles. In Mexico, the brother of Quetzalcoatl, who's dog-headed, is called Xolotl, and he walks backward into the netherworld. I also have a postcard showing St. Christopher with a dog's head carrying Christ across the water. A dog-headed St. Christopher is an orthodox Greek icon. Mercury, the psychopomp, the soul-guide to the otherworld, is attended by a dog.

See, there's a desire that leads us into experience, which leads us "down"—not *morally* down, I mean down into physicality and into the world around us. This is Anubis. He's our curiosity. "I want to know that!" Why? It's our *personal* desire to experience wisdom. Behind this lies Thoth, the God of Wisdom, who knows all the answers already; Hermes is the Greek name.

In the judgment scene that we talked about earlier, Isis is shown touching the dot representing the sixth chakra on the support pole. And she's pointing to it to indicate that she *is* wisdom (the simplistic designation of that chakra), and hence at the Judgment of the Heart she reminds us that the judgment is based not only on factual truth (that is, Thoth's objective truth) but also on the truth in or of the soul, in which love and mercy are considerations in spiritual evaluation.

The heart that is being judged is the fourth chakra, and four is an even number and thus feminine. Which is why the cry that the person being judged utters is "Heart of my *Mother*, Heart of my *Mother*, do not find or witness against me," etc. It doesn't say, "Heart of my *Father*"! It's not just objective truth and objective wisdom; it also involves the subtlety of the feminine nature with its love, its attachment, its qualities of the soul. Because the heart is a meeting point between the higher and lower natures.

But let's not forget about the dark side of Isis! In *The Contendings of Horus and Set*, the goddess sometimes comes out on the side of Set, and Horus gets so mad that at one point he cuts her head off and replaces it for a while with the head of a cow. It's as if Horus were saying, "I want you to be docile like Hathor, Goddess of Love." In other words, the *human* head is the one that can sometimes come with evil ideas . . . and Isis is not incapable of that.

In the *Book of the Gates*, a New Kingdom funerary text, we can observe at the doors of the chambers, or hours, a series of goddesses: "She Who Guards (the Fiery One)," "She Who Guards (the Brilliant One)," "She Who Guards (the One Who Cuts Up Souls)." Every single gate is guarded by an aspect of the Mother Goddess, who's a perfect terror! And think of this from the point of view of a child, for whom each new situation that has to be faced is terrifying, such that life itself seems to be a projection of the mother! The Mother Goddess sets the tasks and challenges.

That's why Erich Neumann in his book on the Great Mother uses a picture of Isis as the frontispiece—because, he asserts, of all the goddesses, Isis is the most universal and characteristic. She *is* the Great Goddess, by which he means she's fundamentally constructive but also has the other side. The "negative" goddess is simply a destroyer; the "sweetie-pie" goddess is not a builder of reality or firm foundations.

We rise up through the realms of the gods, but experience them also. And you can't rise up to Isis and Osiris without going through Set. You have to go through the "lower" experiences—and some do it without agony—but you *do* go through it. You have to come to an awakening of your own consciousness, which entails asking, "Do I care about myself? Do I care about my fellow man? And if I do, how much do I care? What is the nature of my caring? Do I have aspiration?

Do I coast and let other people do my thinking for me?" For if you pursue truth, how much falsehood can you put up with? The Egyptians were always trying to live up to what they called Ma'at, right order. It was based on the rising and setting of the sun, moon, and stars, the rise and fall of the Nile, the cyclicity of nature. And we give offerings and food to the gods in order to give them strength, so that they can intervene on our behalf. There's a reciprocity between them and us. But of all the offerings, devotion is perhaps the greatest.

8

THE ISIS/OSIRIS

WORKSHOP:

Evangeline and Franklin Kane

Franklin Kane. Edmonton, Canada, 1993

Evangeline Kane. Edmonton, Canada, 1993

*I*n May of 1990, I received a letter from Evangeline Kane, a psychologist living in Edmonton, Alberta, Canada. She had read my book *In Search of Omm Sety* and mentioned that she and her husband, Franklin, a counselor, were making plans for a five-day workshop in which, she wrote, "we shall live and enact the Isis/Osiris story." She wondered if I could locate for her a complete text of "The Lamentations of Isis and Nephthys," from which I had quoted in my book, because, she asserted, "I know many women who are lamenting over their dead husbands, both inner and outer, but they have no sacred mourning rituals."

I wrote back to suggest several English translations of the lamentations, and also to ask if she could let me know something more about the forthcoming Isis/Osiris workshop, which had piqued my interest. Ten days later I received a flier for the workshop, which was to be held in Edmonton in July of that year. "During the workshop," the flier declared, "we shall be employing rituals of dance and drama, color and sound, mask-making and hieroglyphic thinking to enable us to *become* Egypt, 'which is a living metaphor for what is the deepest creative impulse in ourselves.' We shall be embodying the drama of the mythic 'family' in its cyclic deaths and resurrections."

I called Evangeline Kane to ask if I might visit her and her husband in order to find out more about their workshop and their ideas concerning the story of Isis and Osiris. In the early winter of 1991 we finally got together.

Seven thousand eight hundred miles from the Land of Khem lies the city of Edmonton. Once a fur-trading outpost, the transformed, high-rise capital of Alberta is situated in a river valley at the edge of the prairie, an aspen parkland, and a boreal forest. Driving past the Muttart Conservatory, I noticed four massive glass pyramids containing flora from around the world. But the resemblances between Edmonton and Cairo stop with these pyramids; the former city has a population of around 750,000, the latter of nearly 15 million. When I arrived in Edmonton in early November, six months after my meetings with the Ammonite Foundation, it was about eighty degrees cooler than Cairo had been, and snow and ice were on the ground.

Evangeline and Franklin Kane live just east of downtown Edmonton with Nicholette, Evangeline's college-age daughter by a previous marriage, and three cats and a dog in a charming, three-story suburban house on a quiet street that is actually more like a country lane, lined with birch, spruce, fir, and Manitoba maple trees. Behind the house is a large garden, then bare and white but that blossoms with delphiniums, gladioli, poppies, and night-scented stock in the summer. Behind the house, just a short walk through the snow, is a ravine leading down to the river. Amazingly, this magical little oasis is just a few minutes' drive from the futuristic landscape of Edmonton's business district.

The daughter of Salvation Army missionaries, Evangeline Kane was born in 1943 in the East Indian state of Orissa and attended boarding school in the Nilgiri hills. She completed her undergraduate studies in education at Goldsmith's College, University of London, and for two years taught young children in Dorset, then emigrated to Canada with her first husband and earned her post-graduate degrees in educational and imaginal psychology. Drawing on her work with incest victims, she published her first book, *Recovering from Incest: Imagination and the Healing Process,* in 1989.

"When I arrived in Winnipeg," she recalls, "my first husband and I had a friend, a very unconventional rabbi, who invited us to visit an ashram in Nelson, British Columbia. We went, and there was a nice bookshop there. I opened up a volume—Jung's book on dreams—and the first thing I noticed was a picture of Ganesh, the Indian elephant god, who has always fascinated me. Part of my personal mythology is that I was conceived from an elephant—that's the story that went on about me where I was born! So I said to myself, 'What *is* all this?' And of course that's the question that I've come back to and that I've found meaningful. But I guess I first had to learn how to allow myself to practice the art of symbolic thinking, which took me to the work of D. W. Winnicott and Melanie Klein, as well as to Jung and to ancient Egyptian theology."

The son of an immigrant Ukrainian Jewish family, Franklin Kane was born in 1938 in New York City. "If you think of a tension of opposites," he says, "then Evangeline's and my backgrounds are just that." Influenced by Rudolf Steiner's anthroposophical and educational ideas, he took a Waldorf teacher training course in England after completing university. "Over there," he remarks, "I was working with children who were tough, abused, and emotionally hurt, and there was no psychological therapy. What there was was painting, modeling, eurhythmy, singing, strong rituals, doing farm work, going to bed by candlelight— and *this* was creating the health-giving situation, rather than self-conscious analysis and formal therapy. It felt right, even though it wasn't in my background."

For more than twenty-five years Franklin was a grade school and high school teacher, a trainer of Waldorf school teachers, and one of the cofounders of Rudolf Steiner College. In 1981 he moved to Edmonton, and later he earned a master's degree in counseling psychology, specializing in imaginal and archetypal psychology. He stopped teaching shortly after his fiftieth birthday to begin his career as a therapist. In that same year he published his first book, *Parents as People: The Family as a Creative Process*, which he dedicated to the children of his first marriage and to the daughter of the woman he met in 1981. "I was still teaching at a Waldorf school in Edmonton at that time," he says. "Evangeline came in one day, and we noticed that we were both reading the same book." Franklin recalls the book as *Descent of the Goddess*, by Sylvia Brinton Perera. They were married in 1983.

The Kanes have individual therapy offices in their home. Evangeline's office, a large, L-shaped room with couch, chairs, tables, and a desk that looks out on the garden, is on the third floor. On walls and shelves and in nooks and crannies, the room is filled with an array of surprising objects: plastic figurines of soldiers, knights, and a sandcastle; dolls and stuffed animals (a lamb, a fox, and a donkey, the last a representation of Lucius in Apuleius' *The Golden Ass*); masks; an embroidery made by Evangeline herself, with this inscription sewn into it: "The spark of life issues from the point of tension created between two perspectives." There are also a little gourd with feathers and a rattle inside, made by the Taos Indians, which Evangeline uses in telling the story of Isis and Osiris in her workshops; clay figures of a small gnome, an ibis, and Athena's owl; the birthday card she received from her mother when she was four years old; a photo of Franklin and herself dancing beside the Nile; a photo of her daughter, Nicholette, when she was seven; a photo of a Tasaday mother gently washing the face of her child in the heart of a forest; and, above the stairway leading into the office, a picture of a scarab beetle, "digging away in the dung," says Evangeline, "and assuring that the sun will rise again."

A floor below is Franklin's office, a narrow room with a sloping ceiling and a skylight. Here, too, one finds a gallery of unusual objects, "objects that sometimes play into my therapy," Franklin says. On one of the walls is a remarkable display of eerily lifelike, sculpted men's faces mounted on wood, presenting the unmistakeable staring visages of a sailor, a Scotsman, a Middle Easterner with turban, and a Mexican with sombrero, among other characters. The room's contents also include sets of alphabet blocks and marbles that Franklin played with as a child ("I play with them now with clients here on the floor"); paper, watercolors, and a board for clients who wish to paint; and, finally, objects from Native American rituals—an eagle feather, Turtle Clan rattles, and a smudge made of sage and braided grass. "You light it," Franklin says of the smudge, "then wash your head, your ears, your eyes, your mouth, your heart, your whole body with the smoke. I have several Native clients, and they think it's important. Would you like to try it?" I nodded, so he lit the smudge with a match, and as wisps of smoke appeared, he brushed the smudge over both himself and me. The scent was irresistible, the effect meditative and calming.

When I visited Evangeline and Franklin Kane on the weekend of November 8, 1991, they immediately gave me a tour of the house. Refreshed by my smudging, I joined them in the warm, cheery kitchen, where we sat at the large center table, drank many cups of herb tea, and conversed for two days, with occasional visits from their dog and cats. After a long, bracing walk down the nearby ravine, I looked out the kitchen windows at the clear, hard-edged northern light, the trees laced with snow, and, flashing by, jays, magpies, and ravens. As the three of us discussed Isis and Osiris, Evangeline spoke in a passionate tone, with a distinct Brit-

ish accent; Franklin in a soft and compassionate voice, with Amer-
ican-Canadian exactitude. Far from Egypt, the ancient mysteries
were alive in this Edmonton hearth.

You told me, Evangeline, that your parents were Salvation Army missionaries.
What happened to change your way of looking at things?

E: I fell out of the Judeo-Christian paradigm one day when I was
a student, when I had the shocking experience of trying to pray
and found that nothing meant *anything* to me. It was so painful to
realize that I no longer understood those words that I had said
for two thousand years, so to speak. I was traumatized. And my
pathology of needing to be excruciatingly honest made me think,
'Since I understand nothing of this, I will no longer pray words
that mean nothing.' It left me with a search for something that
not only would touch me but that I could be intellectually comfortable with.

Like Isis longing to search for the pieces of her husband's body?

E: That's such a nice way of putting it. What that crisis did was
force me into faith in myself. I made a decision that if something
didn't fit for me, I wouldn't embrace it. I suppose in technical
language I'd say that the locus of control began to come from
inside instead of being *out there*. There was a shift in centers.

And Franklin, what happened to change your perspective?

F: Before my early twenties, I had no connection with imaginal
work of any sort. I was just a good, culturally Jewish, Marxist
intellectual. There had been no storytelling in my family life, no

soul nourishment to think of, except for some time that I'd spent with my rabbi, who was a father figure to me. Whatever imaginal work I had came out of the Old Testament, which I later turned my back on. Then in England, when I took a teacher training course in Waldorf education, I discovered that so much of it was steeped in mythology, the growth of the individual child parallel- ing the growth of world consciousness, and I began to notice which stories from different periods of the evolution of humanity were right for children at particular ages.

I started to realize that the Old Testament was also a record of the history of consciousness, reflecting the path of the Jewish people. I began to feel that the limitation of the Old Testament was that it tolerated less and less direct experience of the gods— the *neters*, the spiritual world—and required more and more faith in a demanding God. So I moved away from the centrality of the Old Testament, and from then on I could walk into a synagogue, a church, or a Hindu shrine and feel open to the religious expe- rience of each.

How did Isis and Osiris enter each of your lives?

E: One way was through dreams, the other through reading, find- ing myself drawn more and more into the story, which began to have more and more meaning for me. There's something about the mythology and theology of ancient Egypt that has become utterly compelling. It speaks to me, it makes sense to me, it enliv- ens me, it questions me, it moves me—all those things.

When we were in Greece, after a stay in Egypt, I had a dream in which I was walking around a Greek ruin and was very busy planting red geraniums. And somehow that summed it up for me. There's some blood passion, some earthy green and red passion that's missing for me in Greek mythology. I didn't find geraniums,

of course, in Egypt, but the "vegetation," the green and red opposites—the green of Osiris, the red of Set—are presented to me
there in such a primeval way that they *grasp* me.

I also remember having a dream twenty or so years ago about
Isis. In that dream I couldn't spell her name because I felt I'd
never heard it before. Over the years I kept sniffing around until
I gradually got on track. Having a dream like that is like having
your antennae up, and you feel that you have zeroed in on something.

How did you continue to explore that dream of Isis?

E: It's like falling into a lake. The first thing you think is "I'm
drowning." And then you realize you're not drowning, and you
start swimming, and you say, "Oh, here's this lotus flower, and
there comes a crocodile, so I'd better scramble up for a while until
I make myself a papyrus boat." One thinks about these things
symbolically, and one explores to the extent that one is able to be
touched by the symbol. When one isn't able to be open to the
symbol, one has to come back to the lake again and sit and say,
"How can I relate to this symbol?" Let's say it's the crocodile.
You may think that you don't have a little vessel, that you're not
a little vessel yet and therefore can't encounter the crocodile. So
you have to think how you *can* be a vessel. It's an interchange, a
dialogue, giving oneself permission to play a game. And that
means always being open to new things, new insights, and to one's
own emotional response to them.

F: In 1965 I was living in Sacramento, California, working in a
Waldorf school, teaching eleven- and twelve-year-olds. We were
studying ancient Egypt. I wrote a half-hour play about Isis and
Osiris, and we performed it with eurhythmy, music, and costumes.

I remember spending three days after school with the class making a sarcophagus out of plywood and then gilding it and painting hieroglyphics on it.

I took the class down to the Rosicrucian Museum in San Jose—it looked like an Egyptian temple. Downstairs, in the basement, there was a reconstruction of a couple of tombs. The museum administrator allowed me to take my students into one of them and shut the door and turn off the lights for five minutes. I wanted the students to experience what it felt like to be entombed. I told them that every Pharaoh was entombed during his lifetime—it was part of the initiatory process, and the story of Isis and Osiris was part of that initiation, since one couldn't become a Pharaoh without an understanding of it. Well, being in there with them was one of the most powerful experiences in my life as a teacher. The kids came out transformed. My connection to the Isis and Osiris story actually goes back to that point, where I too began to experience the myth, not just teach about it.

What aspects of the Isis and Osiris story interest you the most?

F: It depends on which day you ask that question—it's really that simple. There are so many motifs in the story. To me, it's the story of the archetypal human being. You can draw from it almost any psychological or philosophical issue. It's a seedbed for almost all the archetypes. The wonder of it is that so much is contained in just one story.

Right now, the theme of red and green, of the dark and the light masculine, is very rich for me, because I do a lot of work with men in my practice, and the subject of combat and competition between two men comes up quite often. What is it to be Setian or Osirian, red or green? In our Isis/Osiris workshops, we've done painting exercises using red and green, which are complementary colors. If you look at red, the afterimage is green; if you look at green, the afterimage is red. So they're connected but on opposite sides. And we've worked with that as part of the whole Isis and Osiris experience. But in my *individual* therapy it's not that I'm bringing the myth forward; rather, that the myth is speaking through me *indirectly*, working as an image reflecting back into a particular moment of the work or of my own life.

E: And the story embraces the whole life of society. It's how you thresh the grain, how you live with your family. Ancient Egypt *was* its theology, and its theology spiraled very much around the Isis and Osiris story, from politics to the stewpot.

For me, the most compelling aspect of the story is to see how archetypically present the feminine is, in a way that she is not in Christianity—certainly not in Protestant Christianity. I remember one of my patients, when asked about his Catholic background, said cynically to me, "All I was left with was a fucking dead god in his mother's arms!" We just sat with *that* horrendous tragedy for a while! And what the Christian story has left out for me and for many people I work with is the role of the feminine with regard to the renewal of God and the renewal of humanity.

Keeping in mind the Isis/Osiris story, when one sees drawings of a Pharaoh in his tomb, one can see Isis and Nephthys right there beside him. And at a later moment in his journey into his body, into finding himself, one sees him there, in the darkest of night, still in his tomb. But now he has become a cradle, and there's the little Horus standing there; it could be his own phallus renewed—that is, his sense of himself as a man. And the two goddesses are still there.

We have only remnants of all this in Christianity—for instance, when we're told that Mary Magdalene was the first to see the new Christ arisen. What a powerful understanding it is to realize that the old-king energy had to descend into *her* under-world, into the bowels of her being, and there be reborn, and that she's there really to assist in the birth of the new man. To encounter that Egyptian mythological appreciation of the feminine we as women carry, or *can* carry, is a truly amazing awareness.

When you get close to the Christmas story, the same theme appears: the precious new baby is born, and Herod, or Set, is out to do away with him. And where does the Christian holy family go? To Egypt. To the Nile Delta. Why the Delta? In the Isis/Osiris story, that's where Isis went to protect her child. And there Isis stayed, in seclusion, away from the destructive masculine, if you like, away from that intrusion that attempted to kill her new child. And who looked after her there? Her friend Anubis, the jackal-headed god. And Hathor—a marvelous goddess: she's Aphrodite, the Great Mother, and the celestial cow up in heaven *and* down on the earth. What wholeness! It's not there in Christianity.

I remember years ago having an incredible dream in which I saw Osiris arise from his tomb, the bandages were coming off him, and he came to me in marriage. Yet, strangely, he wanted to strangle me, and funnily enough at that last moment I just yielded to it, and instead of him strangling me, his wedding ring slipped off his finger onto mine. (In fact, that "ring" became my actual ring, which I designed and which I wear all the time to remind me of my inner Osirian connection. [E. now shows me her beautiful ring—a spiral gold snake with a ruby from southern India.] And *that* to me is my *inner* relationship to that arisen male—not of the upperworld but of the underworld. That underground male god that is also not valued in Christianity. We don't know the tomb experience of Christ, his underworld experience. We know more about the tomb experience of the Pharaoh. I think that as we allow ourselves to be affected by the Christ archetype, we have to ask what happened to him when he entered hell. What was that profundity? And that, to me, is the whole process of psycho-therapy—to learn to become open to the underworld.

What do you think it means that Isis, Osiris, Nephthys, and Set are all brothers and sisters?

F: For the Egyptians, it was important to distinguish the gods from human beings. One of the universally basic taboos is incest, because if we fall into our mother's, sister's, father's flesh, then there's no consciousness, there's too much sameness. And part of the taboo is to control something that's very instinctual, which is to literalize our first love. Here in this story, they're all brothers and sisters. Osiris, who's married to Isis, has had an affair with Nephthys, and Isis with her father. The gods are all bound together, and there's a certain lack of consciousness manifested in them.

E: One of the things that has fascinated me about the birth of the five gods—there was also Horus the Old, don't forget—is that they were born in a gap between the years. A year had 360 days, then there was a gap, and that was the time in which the gods were born. Now, if you and I are so enmeshed that we really can't see each other, then we have to find a gap into which the gods and goddesses can be born within the vessel of our relationship. And then we can commune. Because when they're present, we're not merely battling egos. There's a divinity *between* us and *within* us. And it was the same with the Nile River, the source of life—*it* came through a gap. I often say to my clients, "The Nile came through two huge rocks, and when you feel you're stuck in a place of terrible tension, between a rock and a hard place, that's the very moment when something magical can come through." Most of us tear ourselves off the cross, from that point of tension, and run away. But if we can keep breathing and let the river flow, then those gods and goddesses come down the river, and something begins to change within us.

Now, of course, I'm talking in a "story" way about how I've come to look at object-relations work. Here we are as psychologists trying to talk about how people can develop their sense of inwardness, their sense that they can be at home in themselves, with a space around them *and* in relationship to someone else. If we're closed up in pathology we're just locked in ourselves, and yet there isn't really a sense of inwardness, and neither do we feel comfortable with someone else. We're either enmeshed with them in some way or totally armored off from them. The Isis and Osiris story talks about this very profoundly. When the new child Horus is born—the capacity to relate to symbol and the Other—you see him sitting in the lotus, contentedly sucking his thumb. (See Illustration 8.1.) Of course, we moderns might call this his transitional object, that early experience which allows him to have an objective relationship with the other. It isn't that he objectifies the other but that he is enough his or her own self so that the other reality can *also* exist. And in adulthood, just as the gods and goddesses can live, so the other person can live with his or her own complexity. I don't think we've got a deeper level of understanding about object relations than that which we find in the story of Isis and Osiris.

F: True love does not come with enmeshment, it comes when two separate individualities come together, each recognizing that the other is separate from himself or herself. Osiris remains Osiris, Isis always remains Isis. The first moment is enmeshment, and it's fine as a first step. It's the infatuation . . .

E: And you hope it gets you through your childbearing years!

8.1: The sun god as a child on the primeval lotus. C. 44–30 B.C. Armant.

F: And your own infantile state.

E: Because otherwise women are left abandoned to raise babies by themselves, which is not a good state of affairs. However, it's very important to "fall in love"; and while it's "working," nobody should just call it projection, because it's a time when one *is* open. When you're in love, you can usually *hear* somebody say things about your sensitive points, whereas a few years down the road you can't or won't hear. Look at Isis and Osiris—they came out of the same womb. And that was fine for a while.

F: Yes, they were said to have loved each other *inside* their mother's womb!

E: Then, you see, they were born into human consciousness. Now in a way, the gods and goddesses *aren't* conscious.

F: They don't have freedom, really. To a great extent they *have* to do what they do. And our task as human beings is to disobey the gods, to make mistakes, and to go on from there. And this story is already pointing the way to bring value to making mistakes.

E: The gods enter our beings because we enter relationship with them. At a symbolic level, we can start telling them how we see things . . . and that opens up their blind eye to the human perspective.

In what sense would you say that the story of Isis and Osiris is a love story?

F: Evangeline used to point out to me that in certain old family photographs you very often saw the man staring at the camera and the woman staring at the man. Certainly, in almost any relationship far more energy is being given to it by the woman. So Osiris goes off to "civilize" the world, and Isis has to guard the back yard. When he's defeated by Set, she has to put *all* her energy into the relationship. And where is he? He's in the underworld. So often he's "out there" and she's somewhere else. The devotion of Isis is classic—she doesn't stop. She can overlook all sorts of problems that would be big stopping points in a human relationship in order to do what has to be done. And this even when she's not being fulfilled, since she's married to a ghost—the "absent father," as we say today! And yet she loves him. With all the tragedy that's involved, it's a profound love story.

E: I think that's all true . . . but it's not just *because* she loves him, it's because she *must* have that relationship with the eventually risen Osiris, who has learned to speak her language of the mysteries of the underworld. So it is central that she make this thing happen, for her own sanity's sake. And it's becoming a prime necessity for women in all walks of life, for their own sanity's sake. It's not just for the love of Osiris that Isis must have a partner who *knows* her world and doesn't just *conquer* it. It's a pressing necessity at the level of the man-woman relationship and the future of our life on earth. And that, it seems to me, is a part of Isis' passion.

In the context of this redefined relationship, how does Horus function?

E: For me, the new Horus is the masculine energy that is born in the woman—she is inseminated by the god in his death, really. Isis collected all Osiris' parts together, but his phallus could not be found, so she "fashioned the phallus," as it's sometimes said. But there is a sense in which a woman in her journey has to find her *own* phallus—and I'm not talking about becoming a man, but about that birth of the masculine within herself, something that happens to a woman in solitude, in her sorrowing, in her being alone in the marshes. And then that new Horus can be born and brought back into the functioning of society and the continuing struggle between Set and Osiris, between the old and new world orders.

When in therapy I see women enmeshed in the patriarchy, in what I call phallic domination, they often picture themselves, at a dream level, as having a phallus. That, in my experience, occurs very early in therapy. It usually is a time when a woman hasn't separated from pretransformational Osiris, when she hasn't gone through the pain of disconnecting from the patriarchy that she has hung on to in the hope of attaining some self-esteem. And of course it doesn't work.

Isis finds her own relationship to the masculine. She develops an independent relationship to the phallus. We don't see it because it isn't hanging on her being, she isn't *sprouting* it. It's a hidden yet potent thing. Having redeemed herself from the old relationship to the patriarchy, where there's always a mixture of enmeshment and hatred, she can now give birth to the new masculine herself. She no longer needs to hang on to her feelings of hostility toward men, because she can see the difference between the "old" and the "new" man. She can also see the suffering of the "old" man, even though it's often well camouflaged.

F: For me, the new Horus poses problems for men. He is fatherless, having only a ghost of a father, and his training from Osiris is to prepare him to be a warrior. Only much later, after his monumental battle with his uncle Set, does he become something more than an adolescent warrior. He must first experience victory and then humiliation. Only after he is prepared to sacrifice a part of himself does he become a full man, one worthy of being a king in the sense of myths and fairy tales, where "king" means a man in his wholeness who has strength, courage, and wisdom. It's that basic masculine dilemma of being the outer hero and at the same time having a rich inner life.

Osiris is the hero in the distance. But one might also see *Set* as the hero. He's not a *nice* hero, but he's a hero—he's macho man himself, the hero gone bad. All he's interested in is power and conquest and victory and subduing his brother and taking over the world. And in a certain sense you could look at Horus as someone who's being groomed to become that kind of hero. The key question asked of him is, "What's the most important thing you can hope to do?" And his answer is "to avenge my father."

E: And mother!

F: And mother. And what's the most important animal for him to have? He chooses a horse so that he can chase down his enemy. He's almost the hero incarnate. It's also interesting to mention that his upper body is developed but he has weak legs, as if he's not grounded, not connected to the earth. But he comes through the combat, and he *is* a hero. Toward the end of the story, however, there's a transformation he has to go through so that he can truly serve the gods, truly serve Osiris—sacrificing his left eye, the Eye of Horus, as an offering to the mummy of Osiris, which gave to that god an eternal life. In comparison, Set never gets past his passions, he's the masculine god gone rampant—and he can only rule the desert. Though at the end—and only at the end—his energies *are* harnessed, and he becomes a god whose decomposing and destructive powers are needed: there can't be movement unless he's there. In this field of opposites, his is a very important aspect.

E: I think that seeing how Osiris is undone by his brother is very important in redressing the Christian myth, which tries to suggest that men are always undone by women. Women have labored under men's shadows, and getting out from underneath them allows women to start exploring what *their* shadows are really like. It allows women to stop being eternally seen as that "castrating bitch" or that evil witch or seductress. And it enables men to say, "Boy, my *shadow* really got me by the balls and undid me."

F: Just think of the colors representing Set and Osiris, red and green. If I shine a red spot and a white spot so that they converge, the shadow that those two lights cast will be green. And if you take a green spot and a white spot and cast them at something, you'll wind up with a red shadow. Osiris is the shadow of Set, just as Set is the shadow of Osiris.

E: And Franklin's image here is important, because it's not just the red light shining in the spotlight, it's really the white light which we could say is the insight or consciousness coming with that redness that produces the ability to see the other side.

F: Without the awareness, we simply encourage an unconscious acting out, which is our shadow.

E: Osiris was castrated by his brother, not by his wife. And when I work around this issue in therapy with men, it's a tremendous learning for them to stop accusing the women they live with of what their own shadows are actually doing to them. So often it's a man's shadow that undoes him at a crucial moment—a moment of celebration, for instance, as in the story of Isis and Osiris. A party is going on, and the shadow comes in and undoes the god. But in a way, it's a kind of fortuitous fall, since Osiris falls into his own body, his own self.

This is the place where Osiris gets his phallus back—but only in the very depths of the night, when he is still in his tomb. In Egyptian paintings you'll often see a little image standing on Osiris' tummy—an omphalos, if you like—but it's really the newborn Horus! (See Illustration 8.2.) From an intrapsychic point of view, this Osirian newbornness, this potency, symbolizes a new relationship to soul—I'd call it intercourse with soul. It's the spark of gold in the darkness, enabling a man to be potent in the realm of soul and not be undone.

So Set is the necessary antagonist, the necessary shadow?

8.2: Horus emerging from the corpse of Osiris, the sun disk behind him, in the burial chamber of Rameses VI. C.1142–1135B.C.

E: I've had the experience of working with men who have been in prison for violent crimes, and I've had a few of them tell me their dreams. And in their dreams they are Osiris—they are men who are doing good things and walking through rose gardens. As Jung said, it's very possible for morality to slip right down into the unconscious. If you think of the Setian archetype in our Christian culture, it's been locked away, not in the desert but in the prisons and mental hospitals. And many of those prisoners can see through to the dishonesty of many of us professionals who think we're so together but who haven't really dealt with our shadows . . . and we make those damned people carry our shadows for us. We can say, *"We* don't need a relationship with Set," but we *do* need Set, because actually, if we truly embraced him, he'd wake us up. Usually we don't like to think that.

F: When I first see clients who are in the throes of a tremendous crisis, they've met Set in some way. If they then decide to continue therapy and get serious about the process, they will change the way they look at their open wounds, going into their depression to work through it. That Setian impulse started it off, that awakening. And it's this process that gets Osiris off his Apollo-like, sun god/inflated hero's journey and into the tomb. You have to enter the tomb in order to be reborn. There has to be a transformation, otherwise Osiris would just go on and on, shedding light all over the world. And where would the darkness be?

Exactly what kind of love story is the story of Isis and Osiris?

F: As I said before, Isis and Osiris are in love in the womb. And I took this to mean that their love was, in some sense, unconscious.

E: That original, paradisiacal state ends when Isis and Osiris are born and become separate. For me, then, the whole journey is to ask, "What does it mean to love someone else?" Which is very different from just being in that romantic place that we all yearn for, since one feels so enlivened by being allowed to return to the paradisiacal garden. There *is* something overwhelming about it. But it is at that point that the journey of learning how to really love someone begins.

This is something I think about every day, and the more I think about it, the less I know about it. What I am learning is how incredibly difficult it truly is to love someone else. Which means that if I go through a conversation with Franklin that upsets me, I have to come back to myself and ask, "What has this triggered for me? Where is my shadow? Where is my rage? Where is my hurt?" It's an incredible process. And that to me is not necessarily loving the other person; it has more to do with being willing to live with the question "How can I love you?" So if we can honestly learn to live with that question, then we have a chance of a marriage.

F: We're told what a profound love Isis and Osiris have for each other, but we aren't given the intricacies of that story as we would be in more recent literature. In ancient times, that may not have been as necessary as it is today. Then, the social, familial, and religious institutions helped support relationships and the individual. Now it is like being in the desert. We have little support, we are thrust out alone and have to face ourselves and create our own support systems. We have so-called freedom, which means that the "devil" has a playing field. The gap in the story is where our devil, our shadow, and our love compete and play. This allows for the possibility of real love in the context of relationship.

E: The "profound love" of Isis and Osiris is one of the gaps in the story. We don't really know what their life is like when he has come back home and they sit at breakfast and eat their ginger marmalade together. What was it like?

F: We're told that it was great, it was wonderful. Why not? That wasn't so much the issue then—though it certainly is now.

E: There *is* something that's infuriating about it, Franklin. It *is* infuriating to be born. I mean, who wouldn't want to have this never-ending love affair in the paradise garden? And there's also something infuriating about the gap. Because I do think that's where we're stuck right now in most of our relationships. There's something we're all searching for, and we can't not have whatever it is. So what can we do? We come to this gap, and this great love story doesn't tell us anything much about what it's like. For me, where I see possibilities of experiencing moments of paradise-in-the-gap is when there is that communion at an *imaginal* level. In other words, when you can get to that place where you're working with body, image, feeling, and personal history. When these all come together, it is in those special moments *between* time, when the gods and goddesses were born. To experience those moments of love, of wholeness, when truly your heart is open; to experience true communion and renewal.

F: Yes, and it is truly frightening for most of us men to stop our forward motion, our outer tasks, and take off our armor or uniform. We feel safer taking care of the Other than being in relationship, which means being vulnerable. With Osiris, it is his *death* that allows him to be vulnerable.

Isis had to undergo her own sacrifice.

E: Yes. And the reason Isis could do that was that she was united with her sister Nephthys, and both of them were at home in the territory of the tomb. So it seems to me that a woman can only make a sacrifice for that Osirian "globe-trotter" insofar as she knows the tomb for her own place and has come to respect it as a place of disintegration and rebirth. For until she has devotion to that place, she will never have the emotional ability or the tools with which to develop that devotion to her husband, whether it be an "inner" or an "outer" husband. She just will not be able to do it.

So modern woman's first job for herself is to find the tomb and to learn to love it, which entails healing her wounds with both *her* mother and *the* Mother, the Great Mother—the tomb, the womb. Many modern women have hatred for their own flesh and the depths of the feminine; that healing has to happen first. And that's a struggle for many women—walking that sacrificial line. If you go one way, you fall into sheer masochism, which is, as far as I'm concerned, *not* okay. There's been far too much of that. And if you go the other way, the danger is that you'll be rescuing the man from dealing with some of his own pathology, which is not right either. It's a very fine, delicate line to walk: "Am I willing to make a sacrifice for that globe-trotter?"

Osiris as globe-trotter?

E: You probably hear my anger and sarcasm coming through. I can understand the point of Osiris' journeys, and I am well aware that Isis ruled most competently when Osiris was away. But I think the feminine and women have been very much left alone in the wilderness by that globe-trotting kind of hero. It does very bad things for the female psyche to be continually abandoned and devalued. For me, the story rings true at that level: Osiris is *not* there with Isis. The ways present-day women can respond to that are legion. And what many of us have done is also to climb up into ivory towers and abandon our own place on the earth. One is eventually plagued by a searing loneliness for the earth consummation, and one can become dried up and very bitter, very caustic—which doesn't help anybody.

F: The point Evangeline is addressing raises a lot of problems for me as a man. We can make fun of Zeus when he goes out fertilizing everybody, or of Osiris out there "in the distance." But if we take a look at these occurrences as part of the creation myth of a particular people, one can see them as aspects of the creative god having to go forth and cast his seed and civilize the world. I'm talking about this now on the mythical level. And when modern consciousness takes that story and personalizes it and says, "Wait a minute! Look at these women who have been abandoned, look at that *puer* hero," it overlooks the fact that this was originally a creation myth. Something had to *happen* out there in the world. So Isis holds down the hearth while Osiris is away in his generative capacity.

We have to be careful not to take this only on a personal level, except to realize that after having been generative "out there" as men, we should be looking at how to be generative *within* the hearth and in relationships. That's where many of us fail. If that hero stage goes on too long and we get too inflated by it, that's when the problems occur.

E: I agree that there's an inseminating necessity for the male spirit which degenerates to globe-trotting, and this is because we haven't lived the Isis and Osiris story, which is one of the reasons it's so essential right now. To me, globe-trotting means easily slithering over the details. You fly from London to Berlin and you never see anything. But if you're one of those damn *things* on the earth, you *want* to be seen. It's the slithering over the complexities of reality that drives women and the feminine crazy!

Here we have Osiris casting his seed out and not knowing exactly where it goes. The sower passes very quickly. Now, if you can imagine being that field and receiving that seed, isn't there a sense in which you might find yourself wondering, "Gee, I wish Osiris the farmer didn't come and go so quickly, I wish he'd stay a bit longer so that I could find out more about him, and him about me, and what the roots of the grain learn of me as they burrow into me!"

Osiris had to learn the rooting experience in the tomb to counterbalance his globe-trotting. We are all having to learn how to experience "root" truth so that Goddess and God can live together in harmony.

After our second late-afternoon break—an outing to one of Edmonton's farmer's markets for a steaming bowl of local mushroom soup—Franklin and Evangeline ushered me into their living room, where we sat on the couch to watch an admittedly primitive home video of scenes from one of the Isis/Osiris workshops. This one, a five-day event, was given at St. Stephen's College, Edmonton, from Wednesday, July 11 to Sunday, July 15, 1990.

"What was the impetus for the workshop?" I asked.

"Evangeline, Nicholette, and I had been to Egypt in 1988," Franklin replied, "and on our return, we had the impulse to take a group there, and out of that came the idea of doing a preliminary workshop. We had twenty-five people in this particular workshop, some of whom were our clients, some of whom were simply interested in our work, some of whom were just interested in Egypt. And we told the story of Isis and Osiris in a version adapted by Evangeline and enacted by her and me in semidramatic fashion, using simple costumes, a drum, and a rattle. Evangeline and I played all the characters ourselves!"

"We had a clothes pole with our various costumes on it," Evangeline said, laughing, "and we'd quickly be putting them on and taking them off."

On the videotape, I saw the twenty-five workshop participants sitting on the floor of a small auditorium as Franklin and Evangeline, in their various colored robes and with a few simple props, narrated and improvised the story of the gods, somewhat in the manner of a school Christmas pageant. It was a charming, awkward, imaginative recreation of the tale, performed by a dramatic Evangeline and a sonorous Franklin, who, as Horus, declaimed, "I am life rushing on, born from the egg of the world, from the belly of a magic woman. I am the screech of wind, the rush of falcon wings, talons sharp as knives. I am man's heart that remembers the love and the terror, the weeping, the beating of wings!"

"On what day of the workshop did this take place?" I asked.

"The second day—Thursday morning," said Franklin. "On the previous evening, Evangeline and I spoke to the group participants for the first time and told them that we would be leading them through an experience. It wasn't going to be a 'processed' event or a matter of 'sharing our feelings.'"

"What do you mean?"

"Quite often," Franklin told me, "people in a workshop do something and then everybody starts processing it. It comes out as a hothouse experience, when in fact there should have been time to remain inside and be incubated. In this workshop we tried to act on several different levels—presenting knowledge of the past and coming to the image, doing the experiential activity, and then observing what inner experiences emerged."

"The question for us," Evangeline added, "was how were we going to experience a monumental story in the fullest possible way? When one works imaginally, one is not excluding the personal, if one is working well. But I think that one of the problems our society has is that it doesn't encourage real imagination but rather *fantasies*, such that we slip into personalizing in very unhealthy ways. I mean, we could talk about Set and Osiris and then declare, 'The men will now say something about their relationships to their own brothers.' We could have spent a whole *week* on 'he said this' and 'he said that' and gone nowhere. The questions for me were 'How can we perceive a new phenomenon freshly?' and 'How can we *relate* to a myth and live within it?'— which is different from *interpreting* a myth."

On the video, I watched Franklin at a lectern, giving a talk to the workshop participants. In order to explain the proceedings, he turned the sound down and declared, "Evangeline and I had decided that during the workshop, the nights were for teachings and the days for enactments. So on the Wednesday evening you're looking at here, I was attempting to explore the experience of ancient Egypt in the context of the consciousness of human beings evolving over time."

"No mean task!" I said.

"Well," said Franklin, "we *tried*. What I was suggesting in that lecture was that consciousness changes. I mean, we're not the same people at eight as we are at twenty-eight or forty-eight. Scholars sometimes talk as if the Egyptians thought and saw the world as we see it. But I think that we have to become real phenomenologists in the Goethean sense of seeing something as it is. To penetrate through the sensory stimuli and come back to the imaginal realm, to the archetype or archetypes. This is why I believe we should be tolerant of all sorts of interpretations of Isis and Osiris, since they are able to reveal so many different truths."

Franklin gave his first lecture on Wednesday night, and during the next three evenings he and Evangeline took turns speaking on subjects such as *neters,* tombs, scarabs, and canopic jars. On Thursday morning, as on the following mornings, the workshop participants met at nine to begin the day by sitting, facing east, and accompanying Evangeline in group readings to welcome Ra, the rising sun, after which they performed some yoga *asanas.* The rest of the morning was devoted to the Kanes' enactment of the Isis/ Osiris story.

After lunch every day a Canadian dancer named Sigrid Dale led the group in a series of movements and dances for one hour. On the videotape, I observed her articulating the Osirian gesture, the Isian gesture, the Setian gesture; watched the women of the workshop "mourning" the dead with motions based on an ancient Egyptian drawing; and saw all the participants sowing, threshing, and scooping up and scattering bundles of grasses ("a way of incorporating the whole story into our bodies," Evangeline explained).

Every day after the movement class, the group gathered in a room set up for painting, and on the videotape I followed individual experiments with Setian red and Osirian green. Late on

Friday morning, everyone was engaged in making masks. I watched on the videotape as workshop members sat on the floor in groups of two amid wet plaster and linen bandages.

"What's happening?" I asked.

"We were using wet gauze impregnated with plaster," Franklin explained. "And as you can see, one of the participants lay down on the floor, and his partner put the wet plaster on his face in order to sculpt it. His eyes were covered, his mouth was covered, but his nostrils, of course, stayed open. He lay still for about fifteen minutes while the mask dried and hardened. And after the personal mask was completed, the roles were reversed, and the first person helped make a mask for the partner."

On Saturday morning the workshop reached its climax in an extraordinary ceremony reenacting Osiris' mummification and entombment. The twenty-five participants gathered in one of the corridors, carrying sheets, cloths, safety pins, and small symbolic objects (rings, knives, jewelry) that were to be placed in their encasing sheets. They entered a large room and lay down on the floor next to their personal masks. Each person was tightly bandaged. Evangeline and Franklin wrapped up the last two people, placed a mask over each face, and said a few ritual words to wish each one well on the journey.

"Once everybody was enclosed," Franklin related, "Evangeline and I read aloud passages from the *Egyptian Book of the Dead*, interspersed with silences, the rattle of a sistrum, the heartbeat of the drum, and quiet, meditative taped music. We were, of course, in the room the whole time, sitting back to back so that we could survey everybody. Some people found it pleasurable, others the opposite. And one person fell asleep and snored loudly! For us it was a very intense hour of work—in fact, it was like doing twenty therapy hours in a row."

"Every therapy session," remarked Evangeline, "is, in a sense, similar to that experience. Working with the dream is an aspect of working with one's human story, which is always a tight binding. And relating to a dream—staying with the tight bindings of *that*—is what brings you to a point of healing. When we can't relate to the dream, we fly off, abandon the objective reality of the psyche. So one might say that every therapy session is the experience of the bandage—the bandage that brings one into a sense of one's own vessel, one's oneness."

"For the two of *us*," Franklin said, "there was this tremendous feeling of responsibility. You had people in a totally vulnerable situation, lying on the floor, bound. The masks were laid on very gently, but we often went over to see if any of the people were moving around on the floor—and often they were, to attract attention. And we then had to adjust their masks."

"At a certain moment," Evangeline said, "one of Franklin's clients was having a lot of difficulty, so he went over and talked to her while I kept the rest of the group going. I told them, 'You may hear someone crying; just allow it to touch you, let it pass through you, and come back to your own images.'"

"To be completely enclosed within one's shell, deep within one's body," declared Franklin, "may allow for the possibility of some kind of transformation. We come face to face with ourselves because we can't do anything else. And that's the experience of Osiris. When he's finally entombed in his sarcophagus, he loses his willfulness, he can no longer do for himself, it has to be done *for* him. And unless he receives that in a healthy way, he's not going to experience the transformation in the underworld."

"The people in the workshop went on their own imaginal journeys," Evangeline added. "Poems and images came to them, sometimes weeks and even months after the event. One of the participants used a piece of her old wedding dress for her shroud. You see, she was going through a divorce at the time, and she sobbed throughout this experience—she was letting go of that old marriage. I believe that a person must allow *soul* to direct one's reintegration.

"The real therapy," she concluded, "is to engage in the act of creation: 'How can I help Ra over the horizon every day within the small orbit of my own little life?' So whatever you do in your life, if you do it in the sense of living it *mythically*, then you are assisting Ra. And by that you live your life, your destiny. You live within the human restraints of your own tight bindings, yet you live the process of decay and recreation."

9

Epilogue: A Night in a Garden of Spain

*I*n late June 1992 a friend and I were in Spain, driving along the Costa de la Luz from Cádiz to Algeciras. At dusk we decided to stop at a beautiful silver-white beach, mostly deserted, about six miles from Tarifa, the southernmost town in Europe, which lies only two miles from the coast of Morocco. It is an area known for its astonishingly powerful and unrelenting winds—the levanter blowing in from the Mediterranean and the more forceful *poniente* coming up from the Atlantic. They are said to be able to drive people mad, provoking some to suicide. They have also turned Tarifa into the windsurfing capital of Europe.

We walked on the dunes until we came to a stone rampart and sat down. Facing south, we could see the lights of Tangier faintly pulsing across the water, the peaks of the Atlas Mountains high above them, and we could feel the fervid, exhilarating winds besieging and encompassing us like the songs of the Sirens. It was with difficulty that we left that enchanted spot.

Continuing our coastal journey the next morning, we drove through Algeciras and headed along the tawdry Costa del Sol, swollen with condos, snack bars, boutiques, and discothèques. Then we got stuck in traffic like that on an L.A. freeway outside Marbella. Finally I saw my friend off at the Málaga airport and arrived in the resort town of Nerja later that afternoon.

I had been invited to Nerja to spend the night at the family home of two Spanish friends of mine. In the narrow streets outside, tourists wandered aimlessly, buying T-shirts, postcards, and trinkets; inside the house, which overlooked the Mediterranean, one existed in another world and time. In the back was a flower garden and a *huerto*. A blazing pink oleander tree and an enormous white jasmine bush grew in a bower, and it was there after dinner that we all sat in rocking chairs, a breeze blowing, drinking chamomile tea until we noticed the nearly full moon and the swath of shining stars in the dark sky. As the poet Antonio Machado had written eighty years before, *"Junto al agua negra. / Olor de mar y jazmines. / Noche malagueña"* ("Beside the black water. / Scent of sea and jasmine. / Málaga night").

One of my friends picked a handful of white jasmine petals, put them in a bowl, and suggested that I place it next to my bed. "They're supposed to keep the mosquitos away," I was told, "and they smell like heaven." That night my room was filled with the sound of the sea and the scent of jasmine. And I dreamed of a woman with long black hair and green eyes, serpents by her side and petals of jasmine falling around her. She was so real that I immediately awakened. In the darkness all around me, the fragrance of flowers seemed as strong as the winds off the coast of Tarifa. I had only caught a glimpse of the figure, but she stayed in my mind; and the more I imagined her, the more she took on a life of her own.

So I got up, lit the candle on the table next to me, carried it and the bowl of jasmine petals to the small desk across from the bed, took pen and paper out of my suitcase, and stayed up the rest of the night attempting to remember and come closer to the Lady of my dreams.

ISIS (LADY OF PETALS)

1.
Lady of Petals,
gone into Underworld
trying to find the perfect flower—
white or yellow, with streaks
of pink in candlelight—
softer than the linen on your golden body,
adorned with every star of heaven—
mirror on your forehead
serpents by your side—whatever you are called—
Diana . . . Demeter,
Ishtar . . . Isis—
one breathes your perfumed air
through nights of sweetest sleep
until your mirror becomes the sun,
and I wake up—
like a face lost in the light,
like a voice lost in the wind,
like a heart lost in flowers.

2.
This scent—
purer than the odor of your neck,
stronger than the sound of the letters of your name

Inhaling deeply,
holding my breath,
I turn myself into the inside and the outside of your being

This scent dissolving me

3.

By the terrace light
Through the blinds
Of the hotel room
I watch your eyes
Closed all night long
And in the shadows
Listen to the wind
Listen to the trees
Listen to the sea

4.

On a hot night
you bring me here,
to the edge of the sea,
and point to a ghostly aura
(the lights of Tangier across the waters)

Years ago,
across the waters,
I sat with friends at the outdoor Café Arabe
smoking kif in pipes,
drinking mint tea with orange blossoms,
and looking across the waters
toward us in the future

You were only seven years old then,
with dark, wide-open eyes—
staring straight ahead—
and now you leave me here,
alone in this world,
with the trees going mad in the wind.

5.

Whenever you leave
I can't remember
what you look like
anymore

(Only your scent
in the palms of my hands)

6.

They say that God is a bud of jasmine
planted in the heart.
Every night I used to feel it,
coming up from the roots.
I would stand very still in the dark,
my arms outstretched,
waiting in the air . . .
until one night,
from nowhere,
a breeze of kindness startled me,
I started moving
(just a little)—
branches trembling,
petals falling,
scent rising—
and then I closed my eyes,
I let my fragrance take me anywhere,
I heard my heart beat everywhere

7.

Every night,
in humidity and heat,
a breeze sends the smell of jasmine

across the southern tourist towns,
till everything is still,
everyone insensible—
a realm of opiated sighs—
except for those who hold
white and yellow petals
(with streaks of pink by moonlight)
in the palms of their hands
and calmly walk the empty, darkened streets—
holding hands in silence
until each petal falls or scatters in a breeze . . .
as one blows off into the hills—
above the shouts and noise returning to the town—
where one bell-ringing, tired donkey
notices a shining petal lodged inside some roots,
works it with his teeth,
chews it patiently,
takes a breath,
inhales its fragrance . . .
then looks up past his blinders
and watches night's sky opening into light
and sees, inside, She Who Makes the Universe Spin Round . . .
Mistress of the Living . . . Mistress of the Dead . . .
Lady of Breath and Splendor . . . Lady of the Deep—
mirror on her forehead,
serpents by her side:
and She is always smiling,
unending jasmine petals falling from her hair.

Appendix

Those wishing to contact the Fellowship of Isis should write to

> Fellowship of Isis
> Clonegal Castle
> Enniscorthy
> Ireland

Those wishing to contact the Ammonite Foundation should write to

> Western Branch Office
> The Ammonite Foundation
> LB 155
> P.O. Box 140279
> Irving, Texas 75014-0279

Index

ALSO BY JONATHAN COTT

Stockhausen

City of Earthly Love

He Dreams What Is Going on Inside His Head

Charms

Forever Young

Pipers at the Gates of Dawn

Conversations with Glenn Gould

Dylan

The Search for Omm Sety

Visions and Voices

Wandering Ghost: The Odyssey of Lafcadio Hearn

HEMPSTEAD PUBLIC LIBRARY

3 1764 00204 8274

299.31
C

Cott, Jonathan.

Isis and Osiris.

$23.00

	DATE		

BOOK HEMPS
DATE DUE
12 11 20 02

DATE DUE
10-09-12

HEMPSTEAD PUBLIC LIBRARY
115 NICHOLS COURT
HEMPSTEAD, NY 11550
PHONE: 516 481-6990

MAR 1 6 1994

BAKER & TAYLOR BOOKS